KT-558-948

'*Good Girls Do Swallow* is for any woman who's ever eaten chocolate and felt guilty about it, whether she is a size 8 or 16.
Marie Claire

'A book that's as harrowing as it is hilarious . . .
it's a damned good read.'
Bodyscoop.com.au

'A non-fiction Bridget Jones.'
Sydney Morning Herald

'Honest and very amusing. A definite on your book shop list.'
Sunday Telegraph

'Oakes-Ash's honesty is bound to be appreciated by chicks who think they're the only ones who've ever devoured an unthawed cake straight from the freezer.'
The Australian

'If you have a friend who keeps moaning they are "too thin or too fat" – buy them this to shut them up.'
BodytalkMagazine.com

'A black, funny and touching story.'
New Woman

'It's the sort of book where you can curl up with a packet of chocolate biscuits, eat the whole lot and come away without guilt.'
Amanda Keller (Australian comedienne)

'A page-turning read.'
The Sun Herald Tempo

'a dark yet comic account of her struggle for a figure to die for.'
Vogue

'This brave, modern-day Joan of Arc has come out, not from the closet, but the pantry!
Femail.com.au

'A worthwhile and entertaining read for anyone.'
Cosmopolitan

GOOD GIRLS
DO SWALLOW

Rachael Oakes-Ash

EDINBURGH AND LONDON

Copyright © Rachael Oakes-Ash, 2000
All rights reserved
The moral right of the author has been asserted

First published in Australia in 2000 by
Randon House, Inc.

First published in Great Britain in 2001 by
MAINSTREAM PUBLISHING COMPANY
(EDINBURGH) LTD
7 Albany Street
Edinburgh EH1 3UG

ISBN 1 84018 480 9

No part of this book may be reproduced or
transmitted in any form or by any means without written permission from
the publisher, except by a reviewer who wishes to quote brief passages in
connection with a review written for insertion in a newspaper, magazine or
broadcast

A catalogue record for this book is available
from the British Library

Material from pp 175–6 in *Good Girls Do Swallow* has been previously
published in *Minx* magazine.

Typeset in Stone
Printed and bound in Great Britain by
Cox and Wyman Ltd

For Mum, Dad
and Kate

MENU

INTRODUCTION

So you want to be anorexic? Join the queue

WHEN I AM THIN I WILL GET a boyfriend. When I am thin I will be promoted. When I am thin I will have a baby. When I am thin my husband will love me. When I am thin my grandchildren will want me. When I am thin I will be young again. When I am thin I will fit into my casket.

If I calculated the hours I have spent obsessing about my own thighs when I should have been studying or working or enjoying sex, and if I added those hours to the number of weeks I spent weighing and measuring in the kitchen and the bathroom and then if I added the combined sum to the number of nights I have spent gorging from the third shelf of my fridge, the total sum would be over two-thirds of my 30-odd years on this earth. Between the ages of seventeen and 31 I lost over 10 stone (63 kg) and gained 12 (76 kg).

As a woman in the 20th, and now 21st century, I have denied my hunger over and over again in the hope that changing my body would change my life. I am not alone in this denial: more than 95 per cent of women have dieted at some time. Like most of them I have experienced the disappointment of regained weight. It is accepted that 95 per cent of dieters regain the weight they have lost within 2 years but the belief that I would be in the 5 per cent that remain thin forever kept me on the diet cycle for decades. If I could remain thin then everything else would be okay. My parents would not fight, my boyfriend would not leave me and my phone would always ring.

I blamed my inability to pour my twenty-something body into a pre-pubescent-sized snippet of Lycra for the fact that 'he' did not call me. I blamed the reading on my bathroom scales for the fact that the girls went out without me. I was forever asking tape measures and clothing sizes to validate my worth in the world. I loathed any woman who lost more weight than me and won the prize I coveted – the thin body and all it promised.

When I wasn't invited to *the* party I blamed my fat. When I didn't get *the* job I blamed my fat. I watched twig-sized girls on the covers of magazines get the man with the money, the gilt-edged invite to the soirée, the jetsetting jobs with first-class airfare. I told myself it was because they were thin. I convinced myself that if I too became a twig, if I denied my real hunger then I would be rewarded. So I got thin time and time again, denying myself nourishment, using laxatives for weight control and thus endangering my own life in the process. At seventeen I was anorexic, at twenty I was bulimic, at thirty I had binge eating disorder.

Anorexia nervosa (self-starvation) used to be a teenagers' disease. It now affects the lives of three times as many women in their twenties and thirties as it does adolescents. Bulimia (bingeing and purging) is used as a means of weight control by celebrities and mortals alike and about 40 per cent of people with anorexia will later develop bulimia. Bulimarexia (starving and purging), binge eating disorder (compulsively eating vast amounts of food) and night eating disorder (only bingeing late at night) have recently been added to the list of emerging eating disorders as women fight the battle of the bulge, wrestle with impending old age and struggle with their roles in the workforce, the home and the marital bed. There are three times as many people with eating disorders than people with AIDS in the US alone.

When I was anorexic I tried to starve my sexuality from my body. I was not a victim of incest; I had no major traumas when I was young. I just did not want to grow up. At nineteen I was raped, but my Bad Body Image had already taken hold in the schoolyard years before. My group of friends spent lunch hours commenting on each other's schoolgirl bodies while comparing diets torn out of teenage mags and wagging the compulsory weigh-ins at the beginning of term. We embodied the statistics. Seventy-two per cent of high school girls want to be thinner and eighty per cent think that being thinner is better.

At my anorexic best I was proud of my self-starvation and flaunted my bones in lycra and midriffs, asking for all eyes on me. If a calorie passed my lips I stayed home and wore baggy, oversized clothing in an attempt to hide the mammoth body which existed only inside my head.

Advertising seemed to tell me that when I was thin I would drive a convertible with the wind in my hair, when I was thin I would go out with a Brad Pitt lookalike and never be lonely, depressed or unhappy again. But when I got thin nothing much changed. I still lamented the shape of my body. Thousands of exclusive party invites did not miraculously appear in my letterbox and no hero in a shining Lamborghini pulled into my driveway.

I got the body I wanted but not the life I had been promised. I was still broke and driving a car with a roof; I was still depressed, still lonely and still waiting to meet Brad Pitt – and I still thought I was fat!

Psychological testing shows that pictures of thin female models create anxiety, stress, depression and self-consciousness in test subjects. Yet I subscribed to every fashion magazine going, cutting out pictures of models and pasting them on the cover of my schoolbooks, dreaming of long legs and flat tummies when I should have been studying my twelve times tables.

According to *Glamour* magazine 75 per cent of women think they are too fat, and the results of a 1997 large-scale survey stated that 89 per cent of females want to lose weight. Yet the majority of women in both these surveys were an average and healthy size. Sound familiar?

And now Bad Body Image is being thrust upon unsuspecting males. Since the '60s GI Joe has increased the equivalent of almost 16 inches (40 cm) around his now bizarrely muscular chest. Only recently, another eating disorder has been added to the expanding list. 'Bigarexia' affects more males than females and is prevalent in gyms across Australia. The predominant symptom? The sufferer can never be big enough.

Bad Body Image is not an epidemic, it is a fact of western women's life. We are bombarded daily with images of thin, young and beautiful women dripping in diamonds and surrounded by handsome men. On average we view four hundred to six hundred advertisements per day and of these one in every eleven broadcasts an obvious message about the importance of beauty. In 1986 it was estimated that almost 70 per cent of all female television characters are thin, compared with only 5 per cent who are overweight. Imagine the percentage today (think *Friends* and *Ally McBeal*).

There is no doubt that for women eating disorders are linked to sexuality and how we welcome our physical development or fight to keep it at bay, whether we are starving ourselves to prevent the development of breasts and hips or stuffing our faces to hide the curves that mark our entry into womanhood. We wrestle with food when we are really wrestling with our hormones. Some women binge and purge to mask the pain of sexual abuse, some stuff themselves to deter wandering hands while others use

GOOD GIRLS DO SWALLOW

dieting to ensure those wandering hands are touching them.

My mother never dieted, but my friends' mothers did. I thought they were exotic and grown-up and I felt the same when I spoke their secret female language of grams, kilos and calories. It is suspected that daughters of dieters will most certainly have Bad Body Image and will then pass this legacy on to their own daughters. When we see our mothers wrestling with the shape of their breasts or thighs then it is more than likely we will wrestle with ours. There we have it: generations of dissatisfied women beating their bodies with tape measures in the hope that they will be thinner than their own mothers.

I dieted because I thought being thin would attract The Gaze. My life was spent in search of The Gaze and naturally I chose a career in the limelight. Look at me, I'm a radio announcer; look at me, I work in TV; look at me, I know famous people! When The Gaze did fall on me nothing much changed. I still did not like myself very much. I was living the life the advertisers promised and I was still searching for something to make me happy.

The year American women got the vote was the year the Miss America beauty pageant was introduced. Women work the same hours as men and do the same jobs as men but we still do not receive the same pay as men. As a general rule, women are only paid more than men in two industries, modelling and prostitution. It's no wonder we think we need to be thin and beautiful to get anywhere in this world.

The politics of dieting and hunger denial are complex. There are a thousand rules to stick to as you wake up in the morning: lemon and warm water to start the day, body brushing followed by a run, cardboard cereal and a sip of black tea, take the stairs not the lift, salad with no dressing, decline bagels in the mid-morning meeting, munch on carrot sticks, sip on mineral water at after-work drinks, cancel meeting in favour of gym, decline date because of size of thighs, devour contents of fridge at midnight. Imagine life without body obsession and food fixation. All that extra time to do what you want. Scary, isn't it?

If you think the debilitating effects of dieting are restricted to teenagers and young women then think again. Eighty-one per cent of ten-year-olds surveyed in 1986 had been on a diet. An estimated 40 per cent of nine- and ten-year-old girls in America are trying to lose weight.

Those ten-year-olds already know that if denying hunger and dieting won't do it, then when they grow up they can choose from liposuction, surgery, stomach stapling and appetite suppressants. Women in Asia fork out thousands of dollars for face reduction surgery so they can appear like the western women on the billboards. You know those women, the ones who look nothing like the average western woman. Not my average female friends anyway.

The bottom line is that we all die. No amount of starvation, plastic surgery or midnight vomiting is going to prevent that happening. Dieting keeps us, as women, in constant competition with each other's bodies and keeps us out of the boardrooms and in the kitchen (or the bathroom). Female politicians are ridiculed by cartoonists for their body size. Is it their excess fat that is making the decisions in parliament? No. So what does their body size have to do with politics? The number of women working in management and as professionals increased in the 1920s and the 1960s and again in the 1990s. The idealised image presented to women in these three decades was first that of the flat-chested flapper girl then Twiggy and then Kate Moss.

The road out of body obsession is far from smooth. Dieting is a $500 million industry annually in Australia alone and is estimated to be worth over $33 billion worldwide. The dieting gurus have an investment in their diets not working because if the diets did work then there would be no ongoing demand for them. Feed the public the

GOOD GIRLS DO SWALLOW

image of thin, virtually pre-pubescent women, depend on their natural competition to create dissatisfaction when viewing these women and keep the cash register open when they think the answer is dieting. The majority of bulimics report the onset of their bulimia occurred during a period of dieting.

It took me approximately 365 cream-filled pastries, three dozen boxes of Sara Lee croissants, 250 custard slices, 15 family-sized cheesecakes and 215 chocolate Yogo buscuits before I realised I had a problem. Then I tried to diet the problem away. It took me a further 467 tubs of Haagen Daaz ice cream, 82 chicken fillet burgers and 3891 Tim Tams (more chocolate biscuits) to do anything about it.

My obsession with dieting, body, food and flesh got in the way of me living my life. It damaged my friendships, my family, my workplace, my bank account, my boyfriends, my social life and my sex life. If I could have lifted my head above the plate of danishes I was always scoffing then I might have seen the real world around me.

You can live a life free from body obsession. You don't have to spend your days blaming your body when things go wrong. You do have a choice whether to believe in the air-brushed eye candy served up on billboards, by advertisers and on television each night.

You can eat, you can have sex, you can like your body and you can relate to other women in an honest, open and supportive way. Girlfriends are not the enemy because their thighs are thinner than yours; food is not the enemy because you don't know how to feed your own hunger appropriately; your body is not your enemy because you are scared of commitment and believe you need to be saved by Prince Charming.

I have written this book because I know that every thought I have had about my body other women have had about theirs. I am not alone in the beating of my body, my envy of other women and my denial of my own hunger. I am sick of waiting to be thin and knowing I will never get there because, at one hundred and sixty-two centimetres tall, even when I weighed forty-six kilos I still thought I was fat. It's ridiculous sticking pictures of Sarah O'Hare, Elle Macpherson or Naomi Campbell on my fridge when I am always going to be five foot four and Rachael Oakes-Ash. But stick figures of them on my fridge I did.

I set myself up for a life of disturbed and disordered eating when at age six I first blamed my body for life's little letdowns. Breasts that budded before their time, skinny girls' playground taunting and thin blonde princesses who always got their man combined to fuel my body hatred. The gym, along with dieting and purging, kept me stuck on the body hatred loop for what I thought was life. The times I did try to get off the loop I was so scared and confused that I jumped right back on.

Recovery is possible. I know. I recovered. But in order to get there I had to see Carol Brady for the two-dimensional mother she was, I had to break free from my Diet Pals, stop believing in Thindarella, turn my back on the mirror, and leave the light on in the fridge in order to stop punishing myself. Only then was I ready to swallow.

It would be unrealistic to think I will never look at my body in a disparaging light again or that I will never again long for the unattainable. I love shopping and I always want what I can't have. But I have now learnt how to manage my insatiable hunger and accept my body the way it is: strong, healthy and average.

QUEEN DRAMA QUEEN

Dear God

I want to be adopted. Please, please God, make me adopted. Maryanne's parents are beautiful, Susan walks funny and Ariane's a wog. I am so boring next to them; please, I neeeed to be adopted.

Let my proper mother be some real famous movie star with an even famouser boyfriend. She had to give me up because the movie studio forced her to; they said it would ruin her career and she thinks of me whenever she has to cry for the camera.

Please, God, if I am adopted I promise I won't spy on my sister Megan and her boyfriend anymore.

In the name of our Father, His son and the Spirit that's holy

Amen

Dear God

Please forgive me for taking photos of my sister and her boyfriend when they weren't looking. It's just that the door was open a smidge and they were making all those funny noises again and Mum and Dad said they're not allowed to have the door closed and she was really awful to me in front of my friends when she said I was getting boobies and I just wanted to get her back and I know that's why I'm not adopted and I'm really sorry.

I promise to be extra good from now on. I won't throw my school lunch over the balcony into the garden and I won't spy on my sister (which will be really hard because she's been grounded for a month and will be at home all the time).

Amen

Dear God

Can you please send me a black best friend? Please, please, please. Just like Janet in *Good Times*. I would just loooove a black best friend. No one else has one and everyone will be soooo jealous.

So if you can arrange to send me a black best friend I would be really grateful.

In the name of the Father and all that

Amen

Dearest God

I forgive you for not sending me a black best friend. Mum said I should spend more time with Ariane Pappadopoulos and her family. They're Greek and speak funny and all sleep in the same bed.

I have been rehearsing my cooking show in Mum's kitchen and I think I am pretty good now. I have got two cameras, one up in the ceiling corner and another on the wall and I practise talking to each of them in turn, just like on TV. I've even got one inside the oven so when I put the food in or take it out I can talk straight into the camera.

So, you can send the television talent scout to find me now. I am ready.

In the name of everyone

Amen

Dear God

Mum says we are moving house from Brisbane to live in Sydney. My oldest sister is crying all the time; she doesn't want to leave her boyfriend. I told her there'd be other boys in Sydney who she can make funny noises with. She hit me with a school book.

Mum says I can still be an actress in Sydney at my new school. I'm practising crying just like Marlene in *Days of Our Lives*. When I scrunch my eyes up really tight and pinch my thigh I can just about do it.

Please God, let the kids at my new school like me. Mum says I may have to skip a year because the school in Sydney is backward. I don't think I will because then I'll be the youngest in my class and I want to be the oldest always.

Amen

Hey God

Please tell my sister I am not possessed by the devil. She's just trying to get back at me for spying on her.

Don't tell her this but I really don't mind fighting with her; it is good practice for my career as an actress. The actors on television are always shouting at each other.

Amen

P.S. Can you get Martin Johnson to fall in love with me? I think he likes Maryanne instead – do you think it's because I'm so big? Maybe you could stop my chest from growing.

Dear God

Do you think I might really be possessed by the devil? I'm bleeding from strange places and I just found two nipples on one side of my chest. Do you think I have cancer? Please, please make the nipples go away. No one has three nipples, I checked in my Dad's magazines he keeps next to his bed. Please make one of them fall off. Please, please.

Amen

GOOD GIRLS DO SWALLOW

Hiya God

My third nipple fell off and I flushed it down the toilet. You don't think it'll clog the drain, do you? It was only small. Thank you God for getting rid of it. I've stopped bleeding too, God; thank you, thank you, thank you sooooo much. I promise I'll stop stealing food from Mum's cupboards.

Amen

Dear God

I'm bleeding again. God, can you make it stop, please, please God? No one else at school bleeds and I just know they look at me in a funny way, I am sure of it. What is wrong with my body, God? Please make it go away.

Amen
P.S. I won't bleed to death, will I, God?

Dear God

I feel so sad, God. Please let my father have cancer.
    It doesn't have to be terminal. Just life or death kind of stuff – you know the sort: lots of tests, remissions and relapses. If not cancer, then you could have him held hostage in the Middle East for the whole world to see. Oh yes, God, the whole world, that's much more exciting . . . please let my father be held hostage and let there be a broadcast live on prime-time news networks around the globe with shots of me, his distraught

GOOD GIRLS DO SWALLOW   21

and loving daughter, pleading with the kidnappers for mercy. That's what I really want, dear God. I promise I'll be good. I just need a reason for all this sadness, God. Please give it to me.

Amen

Dear God

I can't stop listening to Meatloaf. His songs are just sooo sad. Do you think anyone will ever love me? Then I could have a broken heart and sing songs like Meatloaf. Have you listened to his words? They are soooo beautiful.

I just cry and cry and cry and I don't know why.

I have started at my new high school, God. It's all girls (no boys allowed). There are so many rich girls at this school that one of their dads could be a movie producer and discover me.

Amen

Dear God

Mum screamed at me for stealing the cakes from her freezer today. She found the wrappers under my bed. Please make me stop eating, God; please, please, I'll do anything if you make me stop eating. Please make me sick on Thursday; they are weighing us in gym class and I don't want anyone to find me out.

Amen

GOOD GIRLS DO SWALLOW

Dear God

You'll never believe it. The boys' school is doing a musical, *My Fair Lady*, and we're all auditioning. Even Katrina Rowland, who has never done a musical thing in her life.

I must get in the musical, Lord. I promise I'll stop stealing the Year Nine lunches from their locker room.

Amen

Dear God

Thank you, thank you, thank you. I'm in!! Katrina, Maryanne, Catherine, Andrea and all my friends are in it too. It's so much fun. I get to sing and dance. I have to lose weight before the performance, God; everybody will be looking at me. I've been eating rockmelons and strawberries three times a day.

There's a cute guy in the stage crew. His name is Peter and he's got basset-hound eyes. Is it true that French kissing means using tongues? That is so gross. Please don't let him use his tongue, God; well, if he ever kisses me, that is.

Amen
P.S. They've locked up some girl in detention, she was caught in the Year Nine locker rooms with a lunch bag. Do you think I should confess?

Darling God

I can't believe it, it's all happening now. My very first proper kiss with tongues and all. At the cast party after the show Peter and I sat on the stairs and listened to Spandau Ballet and that's when he kissed me.

And guess what else? I've stopped eating!!

Amen

Dear God

Naomi invited Andrea and me to go to her church fellowship on Sunday evenings. So we went. It's great. All these cute boys go and after we sing and clap we all get to eat and hang out. I'm thinking about buying a bible. What colour do you think I should get?

Amen

Hello God

I am in love again, not that I ever loved Peter, it was just a kiss really. This time with Gordon Blake. I met him at Fellowship. He's a surfer and he's really tall and good-looking. We kiss all the time but when he starts to breathe heavy he always breaks away and says we have to do some bible study. Do you think he'll always be like this, God?

Amen

GOOD GIRLS DO SWALLOW

Dear God

I saw the devil today. I was in the church on my own and there was a dark shape ahead of me. I couldn't make it out but I just knew it must be the devil so I burst into tears and all the older Fellowship guys came running in to help me. They were so lovely and have been ringing me to make sure I'm all right. One of them even dropped into my house and he was the one I really like . . . do you think if I see the devil again he'll ask me out?

Amen
P.S. Did I tell you I have broken up with Gordon? He didn't like my school friends or my parties where everyone was breathing heavy.

Dear God

I have met a new boy. His name is Eric King and the best thing is he's adopted!! Which is almost as good as being adopted myself, isn't it? I knew you'd answer my prayers eventually.

You know we've even talked about losing our virginity together. Do you think it hurts, God? I mean I haven't even used tampons yet and I am seventeen. I will have to lose weight before it happens though. Does it make me a slut if I sleep with him, God? Angela slept with her boyfriend and everyone called her a slut, but that was two years ago.

Amen
P.S. Look, I'm sorry about the marijuana thing but it does make me feel closer to you.

Dear Goddie Darling

I just can't study, God. I just don't see the point;
I want to go to NIDA and be a famous actress; I
don't need to pass my exams for that.

Amen

Dear God

I didn't mean to do it; really I didn't. My body had
a mind of its own. You know what trouble I have
with my body, God, you know that. I am sorry,
God, it felt so right and he really wanted to and I'd
lost that weight, God. I am not a slut am I, God? Do
you think everyone can tell I did it?
    Please forgive me, God.

Amen
P.S. How many calories are there in a boy's white
gooey stuff?

Dear God

Eric and I have broken up. It's only six weeks to
my exams and I just can't eat. I won't eat. How
could he do this? What did I do? I just want to
die. Is it because I slept with him? Or maybe it's
because I put on weight; I warned him it had
more calories than a Mars Bar. Would that be it,
God? Please make that be it, God.

Amen

GOOD GIRLS DO SWALLOW

DEAN CLOSE SCHOOL
LIBRARY

Dear God

I have been losing weight by the bucketload. Please make Eric come back, please God, please. I can't bear it. I won't eat; I refuse to eat until he returns. I could become anorexic if he's not careful. Bring him back, God; please, please, please. How could he possibly not want me?

Amen

Dear God

Naomi called me today. Said everyone had asked her to. She asked me if I was eating. I lied and said of course I was. She was worried I had anorexia. What a joke. As if I could have anorexia – have you seen the size of my thighs? She said everyone was talking about me. I wonder whether they'll keep talking if I stop eating altogether.

Amen

Hi God

How do you think people would react if I died in an awful car accident on the way to my school prom? My dress shredded; sequins mixed with blood on the windscreen; the prom ruined; girls dripping tears onto their taffeta. Everybody would claim to be my best friend. The church funeral would be filled to the brim, Eric collapsed on my coffin of mahogany and gold.

I want to be buried in my aquamarine fifties

dress with my cat's-eye sunglasses and a pink chiffon scarf in my hair. I want my real mother to arrive as they are pushing my coffin into the embers and everyone will gasp when they see her dressed in her movie star gear; everyone wanting her autograph and her pushing them away to get to the coffin before it burns to a cinder. They'd all miss me then, God, wouldn't they?

Amen

Hey God

I didn't get into drama school. They said I had to get some 'life experience'. I know it's really because I am fat. I sucked in my stomach during the audition but they must have seen it anyway. Please, God; make me not eat, please.

Amen

Dear God

Mum says I have to work for my money so I have taken a job as a waitress. I am surrounded by so much food it's a nightmare. The other night I found myself hovering around some slowcoach encouraging her to leave half her meal so I could inhale it out the back near the bins. I had to cover the security camera with a serviette so they wouldn't see me.

Amen

Dear God

My friend from school, Fiona, she's been taking me out in the city and introducing me to some really really coooool people. All her friends think I'm really fun. It's probably because I am loud and buy them drinks. I feel like such a dud next to Fiona. She is so cool and thin, goes to all the right clubs, knows all the right people.

I have got a job with these really cool fashion designers. I get to manage their shop and hang out with thin angular women who smoke a lot. I also get to wear all their clothes and look like Barbie (I wish). Fiona knows how to drink, she knows all the good-looking guys in the bar, she lets me borrow her stilettos and I look ever-so glamorous – do you think anyone can tell they're not mine?

Amen
P.S. I put a lock on my fridge at home but Mum complained when she couldn't get to the milk for her tea.

Dear God

Fiona introduced me to a really cool guy last night, Brad; he's been friends with her family forever. We were at a nightclub and she wanted to go home and I didn't. I think she was pissed off that I was wearing her shoes again.

Brad invited me to a party. We had to stop to pick up some champagne from his house on the way. I'm sure he locked the door to his room by accident, didn't he, God? He tried to come on to me. I told him I wasn't interested and wanted to get to the party. Do most boys keep a gun collection in their drawer? I must ask Fiona.

I had to drive him to a park near the harbour and he went all weird on me, like he was in *The Godfather* or something. He did some terrible things to me on the bonnet of my car and wouldn't let go of my hair. I didn't ask him to, God, I promise, and I was too scared to ask him to stop. Where were you, God? Does it count if I just stared into space and wished it all over? It doesn't count then, does it? Do you think the bruises on my back will be permanent? I hope I'm not pregnant.

Amen

Dear God

I had coffee with Fiona today and she said I shouldn't say anything to anybody. I didn't tell anyone, God, I promise. They'd just say I was lying; I was faking it; that I just wanted attention. I didn't feel anything at the time, God. I am sorry, God, I let you down. I should have told someone but it's all too hard. Please, God, just get me out of this body. I feel like a rag doll. Make this our secret, God, just you and me, oh and Fiona. Please don't tell anyone, God. It wasn't rape, was it? It couldn't have been, could it?

Do you think he did all that because he heard I wasn't a virgin?

Amen

Dear God

I did it – I got into drama school! Seems I have enough life experience now.

Amen
P.S. What's the world record for eating doughnuts?

Dear God

I couldn't do it. I couldn't go. I'm sorry. I knew they'd find me out. Everyone has to bare their inner souls and dance around naked at drama school and I just couldn't stand them seeing my cellulite.

Amen

Dear God

I booked my ticket today. No one will know me in London and I can be whoever I want to be – who do you think I should be, God?

Amen
P.S. Please get me out of the fridge.

Dear God

London's fab. No one knows me but they will soon. I've lost almost twenty-one kilos. I'd put on more weight before I left Sydney than I thought! Mum and Dad are coming over to England on business, and to see me.

Amen

Dear God

Mum said I looked really skinny. Isn't she sweet? You and I both know I could afford to lose some more pounds.

Amen

Dear God

I'm going out with a millionaire. Well, his father's a millionaire. Anyway, he's heir to a fortune (and a small island in the Bahamas) so I could become 'Lady of the Manor Rachael'. Jacinta will spew. Thank you, God.

Amen

Dear God

The Count (that's what I call him) is so cute. I came home from work today and he was taking a bath in his clothes!! He's got such a great sense of

GOOD GIRLS DO SWALLOW

humour. I didn't want to disturb him; he looked so sweet asleep in the water, so I just cleaned up the empty beer cans and went to bed.

Amen
P.S. Can you overdose on laxatives?

Dear God

The Count wants me to marry him!!! I am going to be 'Countess Rachael'. Of course we don't want to tell anyone just yet (the Count says it's better to wait) but it's soooo exciting.

Amen

Dear God

It's all gone horribly wrong. The Count and I are over. He's been seeing another woman. I can't bear this. She's moved into my room and into my bed with the Count. She moved in the day I moved out and started using my make-up, and my bathrobe! I knew she used them because when I went to pick them up my foundation was open and my robe was wet. How could she, God? I hate her. I just want to die. Please make her die, God.

Amen
P.S. I have lost over seven kilos in two weeks.

Dear God

He didn't notice, God; he didn't notice. He dropped into the restaurant where I work and he didn't notice. He didn't even mention how small my bum is now; he didn't look at my tight legs, my biceps, my flat flat flat stomach, God. Why didn't he say anything?

He's getting married to 'her', she'll probably wear my make-up, and he wants me to go to the wedding! Do I go, God? I could go and look fabulous and then when the priest asks if anyone knows why they shouldn't get married I can get up and everyone will look at me, and I'll tell them all, I will. And he'll walk out of the church with me on his arm and she'll be left crying in her dress.

Make him notice my tight buttocks, God. Please, please make him notice. I don't want to see him again unless he notices.

Amen

Dear God

Mum and Dad arrived in London today. I took them to the theatre and told them I was bulimic. That is what I am, isn't it, God? It isn't normal to take twenty-odd laxatives a day, is it? It isn't normal to eat the local bakery out of custard tarts before 9 a.m., is it, God? It isn't normal to be at the gym twice a day, is it, God?

My mum said she knew all along; but if she knew, God, why didn't she stop me? And Dad said he thought I was stronger than that, but it took me all my strength just to tell him. I have done the right thing, haven't I, God? Telling them, that is. Maybe

I am not really bulimic; maybe I am faking it. Am I faking it, God? Please tell me.

They want me to come home, God, but if I go home I'll get fat, I just know it. Besides, now I am thin again maybe the Count will tell me it was all one big mistake and it's me he wants – and I have to be around for that.

Amen

Dear God

I have been home in Sydney for two weeks. None of my friends even behave as if I was away. Why didn't they drop everything when I got back, God? They paid more attention to Katrina at her wedding than they did to me and I haven't seen them for over three years. How could they do that, God? I starved for three weeks before I came home so they would all talk about me but they looked at her! Even Fiona.

Amen

Dear God

Thank you, thank you. My first job back home and I am a publicist, just like Edina in *Ab Fab*! The record industry is so cool. Everyone wears jeans to work. I don't because my butt looks big in jeans, but I don't say that. I have to act really cool with all the rock stars; please don't let me make a fool of myself.

Amen

Dear God

I've found a really great cake shop around the corner from work. No one else knows about it, so I can't be seen. I would just die if anyone discovered me. Do you think they know it's me stealing the sandwiches from the fridge at work, God? Please don't let them know; I promise I'll stop.

Amen
P.S. Is cocaine natural or chemical?

Dear God

I didn't really like my job with the rock stars, God, but it's all okay now because I'm famous, I'm famous, I'm famous! All my dreams have come true. You are a star, God! No, I'm a star! I get calls, people know my name, I'm recognised in the supermarket. Thanks for organising me a job as a radio announcer. Everyone knows who I am. This is so cool.

Amen

Dear God

Please stop them recognising my radio voice in the supermarket every time I speak. I'm sorry I had to lie, God, but I couldn't say all five packets of Tim Tams were for me – then everyone would know. Sometimes, God, I am terrified someone will catch me out; please don't let it happen.

Amen

GOOD GIRLS DO SWALLOW

Dear God

He is such a spunk, God. I met him in the lift. I just know he's the one, God; please tell me he is. Please make him ask me out, God; he works in the same building and I keep riding the lift up and down and he never gets in. Please make him get in, God, please.

Amen

Dear God

I can't talk. Terrible things are happening all around me at work. I know they're after me; I'm sure of it. Do you think they've found out about me bonking the production guy? You knew about that, didn't you, God?

Amen

Dear God

I've lost my job, God. The guy who works in the building, the one I met in the lift, he was 'let go' too. I know that's a sign, God. A portent sent from you. We're meant to be together, I can just feel it.

Amen
P.S. I think his name is Michael.

Hiya God

You are soooo good, God. Imagine, Michael getting a job at the same place I did. We'll be famous together and sell our love story to *Hello* magazine. I'll wear Armani and Manolo Blahnik and have my own gym and a cook – I want a cook.

Amen

Dear God

It happened. Michael asked me out. We went to see Meatloaf. Only you could have known that, God. It's all on. I'm sure this is the one.

Amen

Dear God

How many joints a day is normal? Is it true it affects the sperm count?

Amen

Dear God

I promise I'll stop ringing him and hanging up, God, if you'll make him want me more please, please.

Amen

GOOD GIRLS DO SWALLOW

Dear God

It's over, I knew it. A girl answered the phone. He's got someone else. I knew it, I knew it, I knew it! Bastard.

Amen

Dear God

Please make him call me; I miss him. I need him to call. He needs to call me.

Amen

Dear God

He called. He's coming to get his things tomorrow. I'm not happy, God.

Amen

Dear God

Do you think he knows it's me making those calls? What if he's got Telstra tracking them? What if he's got Caller ID? What if I answer the door and there's a man there with a subpoena to take me to court for harassment? Then it will be in the papers and everyone will know. I'll be caught out and there'll be photos of me in the magazines and I'll have to sell my story for thousands of dollars because I can't get a job to save myself. I promise I'll stop, God, just please don't let him be tracing my calls, God, please.

Amen

Dear God

Do you think I am a rabbit-boiler? I only drove past Michael's house twice and I didn't even slow down. The same car was there both times. What does that mean?

Amen
P.S. I've lost seven kilos in two weeks again.

Dear God

I hate myself. I can't stop eating, and I mean *really* eating. Please, please, please make it stop. I dreamt last night about Brad, Fiona's friend who took me to his place for that champagne. Do you think that he . . . I mean it wasn't . . . was it . . . but it could have been . . . I didn't say yes, did I?

This can't be happening. I want to wire my mouth shut and sleep for the rest of my life.

Amen

Dear God

Can't talk. Must eat.

Amen

GOOD GIRLS DO SWALLOW

Dear God

I don't fit into anything. Make this weight disappear. I am a mammoth, bloated, huge, big, fat, ugly pig and I wish someone would just shoot me. Pull the trigger, God, go on. Do you think the same number of people would come to my funeral this time? I think pink satin lining would be best for my colouring. But hot pink, God, not baby pink. Baby pink washes me out.

Amen

THE CAROL BRADY SYNDROME

I want to be Rachael Brady. Oops, did I say that out loud?

I want to be daughter to Mike and Carol, sister to Marcia, Jan, Cindy, Greg, Peter and Bobby and best friend to Tiger. I want bellbottom hipsters. I want a shared bathroom and bedroom. I want clear skin and I want a plump spinster in the kitchen baking me cookies, just like Alice does. I want a box on the TV screen with my face in it, a seat in the station wagon and a place on the teeter-totter.

At eight years of age, if I could have crawled inside my television box I would have (I still have a scar on my left elbow from a failed attempt to join the Bradys on their trip to the Grand Canyon). I was there singing backup when they cut their first record, I collected my lunch each morning from Alice and got a mother's kiss from Carol. If I had succeeded in my attempt to get inside the TV during the Brady half-hour back in 1975 I would no doubt have been shoulder-to-shoulder with millions of other pre-teens vying for Carol's attention.

Oh, how I loved Carol Brady, Mrs Brady, mother of me, Rachael Brady. Carol helped me with my homework, drove me to cheerleading rehearsals and combed my hair. I never got my period and Carol always smiled. She never cleaned the toilet because we didn't have one in the house and even if we did Alice would have done that for her. I adored my five o'clock family and my mother's saccharine smile. I wanted to be a Brady because nothing bad ever happened in their world.

Meanwhile back in Real Life Land my mother was screaming blue murder at my sister's substandard school report, crawling out from under the mountain of my father's unironed business shirts and cursing the day the S-bend was invented. My mum was no Carol Brady and like other mothers of the Brady generation she paid dearly for that crime.

Mum worked twice as hard as Alice to be a good Carol, pouring her love into the fridge, filling it to the brim with food to feed her daughters. She'd nourish her girls with casseroles, dumplings, stews, roast dinners and lashings of trifle. There were three of us siblings and we ate for all six of the Brady children.

It's nothing new to fantasise about other people's families, even as the other kids are fantasising about yours. With my mother elbow-deep in toilet drains I dreamt of brown paper lunches, family conferences, perfect hair and chiffon nighties in the hope that the centre of my mother's universe would be me instead of the washing. So I envied Marcia, Jan and Cindy their mother while my friends were envying mine.

Hang around any playground at lunch time and listen in on the kids. 'Gee, wish I had your mum, she's so cool; my mother never lets me ride my bike on the road, and she gives me apples after school, not chocolate bars like your mum does.' 'Have you been to Kelly's house? She's got a pool and a supersonic Barbie with matching convertible AND her mum lets her stay up and watch *Ally McBeal*.'

If the Carol Brady Syndrome was solely responsible for creating my life of disordered eating then every girl who grew up in the seventies would have ended up with an eating disorder. But the picture perfect family on the telly and the envy in the playground did lay the foundation for my obsession with comparing. Once I started comparing myself to others I was never going to be happy. Combine that with a developing body, the rise of the supermodel and my fantasy of emulating Carol Brady's taut thighs in hip-hugging bellbottoms, and I was setting myself up as an ideal candidate for Bad Body Image. Meanwhile other girls were comparing their legs with Barbie's and falling short, or wishing their blonde hair brown, their curly hair straight, their drunk mothers sober and their screaming fathers silent.

Our street (and no doubt yours too) had its very own three-dimensional Carol Brady. Her name was Wendy Harrison, she was my mother's best friend and she lived ten doors down from us. The Harrison home was permanently pristine and smelt soft and sweet and good enough to eat. It was perfect, right down to the two Brady-like children with angel-blonde hair and matching aqua eyes and a manicured mother who baked and cleaned and drove the kids to ballet and softball with a smile on her face. Mrs Harrison's hair was woven in braids of gold and her cheeks were tinged with rose petals. She wore shorts in summer and her legs were toned and tanned.

My mother's nails were bitten down to the core. She wore girdles and her summer dresses covered her knobbly knees. Her hair was wiry and thick.

Mrs Harrison made the best cupcakes in the neighbourhood, perfect clouds of aerated yellow sponge with pink frosted peaks. They nestled between layers of greased paper in Tupperware high on the third shelf of her kitchen cupboards.

My mother's un-iced chocolate cupcakes sank as they left the oven and invariably ended their days in a week-old lunch bag hurled over the balcony into the overgrown garden below.

My mother, her cupcakes and her imperfect home served as a daily reminder of the fairy tale down the road and on our TV screens each weekday at five. I had bought into the perfect image of a united family sold to me by the Bradys. Any house that vaguely resembled the Brady house became perfect in my eyes. I longed for the real life version of the Bradys in the Harrison house down the road. I thought if I lived in a perfect household then other girls would envy my position and I would become the coveted child and that would make me special.

The families I longed for as a kid had their own problems but I never saw past the image presented to me. I believed the hype, I swallowed the myth that the perfect family exists, and once that myth was swallowed I could only berate my own family for its imperfections. I thought I was the only one who cringed when my mother kissed me goodbye in front of my friends or interrupted maths to bring me the lunch box I forgot to take that morning. Somewhere along the line I decided that if I couldn't have the perfect mother and father then surely I could have the perfect body and everyone would know I was different to my family. They might even believe I was adopted.

While I was auditioning for the role of third daughter in the Brady-esque house down the road my mother was working to the bone to make her girls happy. When the Bay City Rollers hit the airwaves she cut up my jeans and ran up tartan turn-up pedal pushers in an afternoon. I wore them out on the street, glowing in the knowledge I was the first in our neighbourhood to don such a pair.

When my sister Megan brought her high school friends home for parties in the billiard room Mum would fry up jam doughnuts by the shuttle load for the masses downstairs. She served my other sister, Jacky, tablets in teaspoons of sugar to soothe her sunstroke with never so much as an 'I told you so' and she cried when the last of our dog Misty's ten puppies was sold to a good home. But all this wasn't enough. I wanted more. And so I screamed and stamped my foot and demanded the Brady fantasy and my mother struggled to say no.

I wanted to feel what perfection was like and when faced with the prospect that my family was anything but perfect I chose to steal the fantasy from down the road.

Each afternoon after school I stared wide-eyed at the top shelf in the kitchen of the Harrison house where the fairy pink icing-covered cupcakes lay in wait. Sometimes I would pull a stool close to the cupboard and, when I was sure no one was looking, I'd climb up and steal a look under the Tupperware lid, inhaling the sugar aroma. At times I was more daring, reaching in and grasping the cupcake between my grubby fingers, pushing the perfect pink sponge into my mouth. I was always terrified that I would be caught out.

We've all had those experiences where we go ahead and do something forbidden knowing full well that we'd be badly busted if we got caught – sneaking a look at the photos under your brother's bed, looking for fifty cents in the bottom of Mum's handbag. The difference was I was doing it in someone else's home. I was stealing someone else's food because I wanted the perfection it promised. I didn't get it, but it didn't stop me wanting more. The cupcake in the Harrison household is my first memory of compulsion with food. I had to have that cupcake and nothing was going to stop me, not the fear hammering in my heart, not the prospect of being dragged home a thief.

If I had been caught Mrs Harrison would probably have laughed, reached for the Tupperware and offered me another cake. But I was already ashamed of my hunger. I was tall for my age and this always translated into 'big' when the grown-ups wanted to pass comment: 'My, you are a big girl, aren't you.' I was forever apologising for my DNA. I wanted to be perfect like the Harrison kiddies. Petite, average, small. My growing body wanted more food than theirs but if I asked for more then I was a 'pig' in my own mind.

Chances are if you have a fixation with food you can remember the first moment it held power over you, that time you found yourself doing something you knew was wrong just to get the food you wanted. For some it's the cream buns at the tuckshop and the way they beckoned at noon. For others it was eyeing your best friend's cheeseburger after you had inhaled your own, waiting for her to look away so you could sneak a bite. Or later in life when your boss pissed you off and you found yourself shaking the chocolate vending machine in desperation.

Like most little girls I dreamed of pink tulle and satin ribbons. Each Saturday my mother would drive me to ballet classes at the local church hall where my friends and I would spend the hour pretending we were butterflies floating in the breeze. One Saturday the other girls danced with small wooden birdcages dangling from their fingertips. I was chosen to dance on my own in the centre of the hall as the girls waltzed their birdcages around me. I didn't have a birdcage but I didn't mind for I was dancing solo. I thought I was the fairytale princess and the girls were my maids-in-waiting.

I did not have a wooden birdcage because I was not invited to do the ballet exam (for which a wooden birdcage was a prerequisite). I danced solo, believing I was special, while the others rehearsed their exam routines. No one told me I could not dance. One Saturday I realised I was in the middle of the room not because I was exceptionally good, but because it kept me from bumping into the other girls.

I was not special. I was not even good enough. My eyes stung with shame and I wanted the church floor to swallow me up.

I blamed my body. I had stolen too many cupcakes. I could have blamed my mother because she didn't buy me the right shoes, I could have blamed my teacher because she didn't like the way I looked, I could even have blamed the pianist who played out of time, but I didn't; I blamed my body. I was eight years old and when I wasn't special I blamed my body. It had to be me; I must be the reason I was not good enough.

I never went back to ballet after that. I knew it was my appetite that had let me down, that if I wanted to be a pink princess I had to stay away from the pink fairy cupcakes. At age eight in the church hall I was the tallest of the girls. Not the fattest, just the tallest (or 'the biggest' as everyone always told me). And so began my life of dieting. Looking back I wasn't fat, I was just ungraceful, more suited to rough and tumble than pointe and demi pliés.

That realisation in ballet class could just as easily have happened if I had ended up as the bench warmer for softball or the dunce in the corner at school. It's something that happens to everyone. At some point in my life I was going to find out I was not the centre of the universe.

In our parents' home we may be the brightest, best and number one but in the big wide world it's only a matter of time before we have to face we may just be Little Miss Average.

For some girls it doesn't happen until they hit their teens and their best friend gets the boy they wanted. A quick comparison tells them they were rejected because they have a bigger belly or flatter chest or zittier skin. Whenever that moment comes it hurts. But it's how we react to it that matters. I chose to blame myself for my imperfections rather than accept that was just the way of the world.

By the time I was nine I was a year off puberty and my body was padding itself for the onslaught of fertility. My Grade Four drama production that year was *Oliver Twist* and I was to be the star. Nicola Ballard was my classmate, an exotic creature with almond eyes and hair straight as a ruler. When Nicola smiled she revealed a row of perfect teeth; when she walked she floated (you know the type). Nicola was the Artful Dodger and I was to play Oliver Twist, 'the hungry boy who always wanted more'. Nicola's mother wanted her daughter to be a star too so she volunteered to direct the school production.

As the date of performance drew close, it was time for us to get costumes. Off we went to the theatre hire store where I tried on rags and riches. While I was struggling into a red brocade waistcoat Nicola's mother decided to pass comment on my tummy as she wrestled with the waistcoat buttons. 'Rachael's big for her age, she's been eating a few too many lollies,' she declared to all in the room.

I was mortified. She had revealed my greed to all. It didn't matter that she was trying to push me into a costume designed for a child two years younger. All that mattered was that she had pointed out my insatiable appetite.

I had been so proud to have the lead role in my school production but now all I wanted to do was run and hide. I imagined myself and my 'big for my age' tummy standing on the stage for all my friends and family to laugh at. I was torn between being a good girl and apologising to Nicola's mother for my tummy or venting my grief. My upbringing prevented me from slapping Mrs Ballard around her saggy jowls so I simply retreated and applied extra chocolate cake to my wounds (though I really wanted picture-perfect pink sponge).

Like most kids when I was sick I got soup. When it was my birthday I got cake and when it was tuckshop day I got finger buns. Food was fun, a celebration and a comfort. I was an active child and burnt off whatever I ate. Remember when you could eat breakfast, follow up with a chocolate milk, a bag of mixed lollies, lunch, biscuits, red cordial, dinner and ice cream and your ribs still stuck out? My body grew at a different rate to my friends'. I was always the tallest in the class. I outgrew school shoes each term and looked down on the scalps of last term's crushes.

Every adult felt obliged to comment on my size, 'Ooh, you look much older than six (or seven, or eight).' I became acutely aware of my body size in relation to my friends because everyone kept pointing it out, and like most kids I just wanted to blend into the pack. My body ensured I didn't. In the first ten years of my life I had already blamed my body for my downfall and felt compelled to eat at all costs and I hadn't even reached puberty. I had, however, set myself up for a lifelong pattern of body and food abuse. A pattern that would be cemented in the hormonal madness of adolescence.

OVERRIPE AND UNDERDONE

I HAD MY FIRST ORGASM aged three, thanks to the seat of my red tricycle.

The metal seat of my trike was later replaced in my affections with my father's 'carpenter's horse' in the garage. My sisters rode bareback in the paddock with real livestock but I was content to canter my imaginary stallion. I knew what I was feeling was good and with the canniness of childhood I knew I shouldn't share it around. So I kept my daily rides on the wooden horse to myself.

At age five I towered over the worm-throwing boys in the playground. By the time I was ten I ran faster, climbed higher and punched harder than all the boys I knew. I was either flashing my Bonds cottontails while jumping elastics each lunch hour or swapping World Series Cricket Cards with the boys at the nets down the back. A David Hookes could get me one Joel Garner, a Gordon Greenidge and a chance to bowl in the nets after school.

Saturday afternoons I spent casing my parents' bedroom for a glimpse of the *Playboys* next to my father's bed. When I was sure Mum and Dad were occupied elsewhere I would close their bedroom door, open the bedside cabinet and hold my breath. Pulling the magazines from the second shelf, making a mental note of the order they were piled in lest I leave a clue to my presence. Page upon page of breasts, legs, vulvas, pubic hair, shaven hair, big tits, small tits, brown tits, pink tits, glossy mouths, long nails, wide eyes, blonde hair, black pubes, brown hair, platform shoes, leather, rubber, lace, silk, girls together, girls apart, legs together, legs apart, lips together, lips apart, my ten-year-old eyes bursting. I bragged to the boys about my father's *Playboys*, and they offered me the entire West Indies cricket team for a peek.

I was confused by the bodies of the *Playboy* women. I looked at their long legs and flat tummies and their pert breasts and I compared them to the bodies around me. They did not match up. My mother's body was stretched by three children, my sisters' bodies were blemished with adolescent pimples. My school teachers would not be found in the pages of these magazines. I knew these bodies existed, I had seen them with my own eyes, but I could not see them in my own life.

That same year my own breasts began to develop. They barely resembled the melons between the pages of my father's mags. Instead I saw small plums when I removed my primary school uniform before bed each night. Still, I did not want them and I strapped them in, wearing swimming maillots underneath my regulation check school uniform. Heaven forbid the boys notice my bumps and ban me from the cricket nets for being a girl, I thought.

It wasn't just the boys I was scared of; I was terrified my mother would see them and I cried when my older sisters pointed them out. I felt enormous, big and cumbersome, looking down on my flat-chested Grade Five pals. The earliest developing child in the history of children, that was me, but it was an honour I did not want. My friends were blocking spinners on the cricket pitch or going on holidays with Barbie in her campervan. I was hiding in the changing-room in the lingerie department of Grace Bros as my mother searched the racks for my first bra. I was horrified when the saleswoman stretched a tape measure under my arms and across my chest. 'She's definitely a D,' she confided to my mother as if I wasn't there. 'No training bra will fit her.' With that, she presented me with enough underwire and fabric for a circus marquee. Once it was locked around me my breasts sat to attention, two targets begging for a bullseye from the boys at the nets.

The scaffolding the saleswoman sold my mother was thrown into the back of my cupboard and I went back to strapping my chest down. My mother never said anything. Like me, she was not impressed with my growing body. Neither of us wanted to acknowledge my journey into womanhood; both of us wanted me to stay a child forever. If I strapped them down and ignored the pain of bouncing breasts when bowling in the playground, then maybe, just maybe they'd go away.

Of course I am not the first girl to get her period early or wear a bra before high school. But I went to a small school and stuck out like a sore thumb. I have girlfriends who tell me the story of their first bra fitting. Some tell it with embarrassment and shame, even now. They are invariably the early developers. Other girls tell of the humiliation they felt when their chests remained flat well into high school. We all wanted to be part of the pack in puberty and early or late development set us apart.

I felt like a child, behaved like a child and had a body of a woman. I wanted to take my body into Lost and Found and return it to its real owner. There was a woman walking around with my child's body somewhere and I wanted it back.

I had plenty of women around me as role models, from the Playmates to my sisters and my mum but I did not want to be like any of them. If I became a woman I might end up in the magazines being looked at by businessmen like my father, or worse still I might not end up with a body like those women at all and then no one would look at me.

Breasts became the least of my worries when I discovered bloodstains on my flowered knickers at the age of eleven. My mother provided me with a sanitary napkin and the printed instructions from the packet and nothing more was said.

I felt sure everyone could see the bulging pad in my school briefs and I went crimson when my schoolteacher pulled me out of the playground to have a 'quiet word' to me about the bloodstains on my uniform. She mumbled something about 'being different to the other girls', 'spending less time at the cricket nets after school' and 'going to the toilet regularly'. I told my friends I'd cut myself and went home in tears with my school jumper tied around my waist.

In high school everyone wanted their period. It meant you were grown-up. When you didn't get your period you were considered a child, a little girl. In high school I would have been an object of envy; in primary school it made me a moving target.

At eleven I didn't care for the responsibility that came with changing pads and breasts that boys pointed at in the schoolyard. I felt uncomfortable with the attention my body created from the boys I shared batting tips with, the murmurings from the girls in the bathroom, the taunts from my sisters. Food relieved the discomfort and hid the curves behind layers of fat. Other girls who developed early no doubt wore baggy T-shirts, or kept their eyes on the ground when they walked, or constantly crossed their arms.

Each afternoon I spent more time with the owner of the milk bar on the corner of my street than I did at home. He sold me caramel buttons by the handful and vanilla slices made by his wife. I would hover around the lolly cabinet, counting again the sweat-covered coins in my hand, and he began to take pity on me, thinking I was not fed by my mother, and putting a little something extra in the bag.

Five minutes after my detour to the corner store I was home, throwing my school bag down in my haste to get to the kitchen before starting on Mum's home-baked mini apple pies.

I was not fat but when I looked at the flat-chested girls in my class I felt fat.

When I entered my single sex high school I was surrounded by other big-breasted girls and felt mild comfort. In the changing-rooms I hid behind my towel and stared at other girls' bodies around me. I was relieved when others were bigger, fleshier and dumpier than me.

While I was staring at the other girls in my form, hoping to find a body bigger than mine, other girls were no doubt staring at mine. The late developers were wishing for my breasts, the average developers hoping theirs did not grow at the same rate as mine, the early developers finding solace in my curves.

When an appropriate number of girls in the one school year have started menstruating it becomes de rigueur to speak of cramps, hot water bottles and pads. If you don't know the lingo then you are not old enough to be in the group. And thus the groups in each year emerge. The late developers seek refuge in each others' hairless bodies. The early developers are now objects of envy as the race to become a woman picks up speed. Bodies are constantly being compared, weighed and measured against each other.

At the beginning of each term in Year Seven and Year Eight we would march into the gym, strip off any excess clothing and stand on the scales. The teachers read our weight aloud, the numbers reverberating off the walls with a distinctive echo: 'SIXTY THREE, SIXTY THREE, sixty threeeeeeee'. We would sigh in collective relief when the number was higher than our own.

I used to think the kilos would go on my record for life. I imagined for the right amount of money you could have your records altered to hide the truth. I envisioned school seniors in dark trench coats accosting young girls with a 'Pssst! Wanna buy a Year Seven weight record?' Once you had the dirt on someone, once you knew how much they weighed then you had one up on them. I always tried to be sick on weight day.

Weight day was not the only event in puberty I sidestepped. The first three years of high school were spent dodging invitations from thin pretty girls to parties where there would be acne-ridden boys. 'Of course I'll be there, thanks for the invite, I'll see you on Saturday,' I'd say but I spent the night at home with Sara Lee, John West and Betty Crocker while my girlfriends danced with Stewart, Robert and Andrew. My school friends were practising for their impending womanhood, at the same time I was swallowing mine down in front of the TV.

Not that staying home with my family on a Saturday night was a trouble-free place to be.

I had already begun to see my mother as weak, pitiful, a failure. I loathed the way she spoke, the food she cooked, the clothes she wore and then felt guilty for all that loathing. I was forever comparing her with Mrs Harrison, Carol Brady and my friends' mothers. I wanted to be anyone else's daughter (provided they were blonde, two-dimensional and perfect) but my mother's.

When my mother refused to buy me the latest must-have-you'll-have-no-friends-without-it studded belt I would freeze her out, using Plan A – the silent treatment.

When Plan A did not work I would resort to Plan B – screaming, yelling and crying. Plan B is best acted out in a public forum like the escalator of the local Westfield Shopping Centre or the second carriage of the city-bound train.

Plan C – emotional blackmail – would up the ante: 'If you really loved me you'd buy me this. I can't believe you are my mother; I must be adopted.'

Plan D involved stealing the money from her purse when

GOOD GIRLS DO SWALLOW

she was asleep upstairs (after a while she cottoned onto this one and slept with her handbag strapped to her chest). If all else failed then plan E would see me resorting to favours and niceties to get what I wanted. 'I love you thiiiiiiiiiiis much, Mummy. You really are the best mummy in the world; all my friends say so. You look really pretty today, Mum. These cupcakes are delicious.'

Somewhere between Plan A and Plan E my mum would eventually give in and buy me the belt. I would briefly become the envy of my friends but within days the belt would be lying in the back of my wardrobe with the previous week's bubble skirt, the previous month's winklepickers and the previous year's new romantic kilt in Black Watch tartan. It was all shrapnel from the constant battle to get everything I demanded.

I had girlfriends who never answered back to their mothers, who smiled sweetly and took no for an answer. I felt like the devil next to them.

When my mother said no I hated her. When she said yes I still hated her.

By the time I was fourteen my mother and I were speaking two different languages. I learnt a sixth step to my foolhardy plan, Plan F. 'I'll tell you about me, Mum, if you buy me what I want' and we would barter snippets of information in exchange for clothes, makeup, concert tickets.

I swallowed my hatred of my body, my hatred for my mother and my hatred for the way my life was shaping up by devouring the weekly shopping before my mother had even placed the bags on the kitchen bench. Then rummaging in the freezer for danishes and eating them frozen as instant relief from the fighting, the teenage angst and the loneliness.

So I was going through puberty, nothing new. In a lot of ways I had it easy, I didn't get acne (except on my back), I never got braces and it's not like I didn't have any friends.

Puberty is hardly a novel experience. My mother went through it, and her mother and her mother. So they cried over the Beatles instead of Air Supply and Meatloaf, they begged their mothers for ponchos instead of ruffled shirts. We all get through it and live to tell the tale and we all have our different ways of dealing with it from ignoring the taunts in the toilets to diving headfirst into our homework or puffing cigarettes down the back of the school. We're hardly going to be condemned in court for bad fashion sense and unwashed hair. But I loathed puberty because it made me different, it gave me The Gaze before I was ready and I became a question every other girl asked: am I going to have breasts like that?

At school I was the loud, happy, class clown. The school amphitheatre with its wide steps and open position served as a solarium. Rows of girls sat with skirts hitched up high, ankle socks rolled down, legs splayed outward to the sun. It was here we would compete for our position within 'the group'.

They were arrayed in order. The tall, thin and rich Year Twelve part-time model got the highest step, the insignificant blonde who always got the man sat next to her, the daring nightclubber was on the next step down, the daring nightclubber's best friend next to her again, the daddy's girl swapping between the highest and the middle, the girl on the boys' bus sometimes up high, sometimes low (depending on what goss she picked up from the back of the bus that morning), the sweet ones (middle step) and the not-so-savoury (the lowest step). Ask your mothers, and they'll describe the same girls, the same as the ones you went to school with, because they went to school with them too.

In the amphitheatre we gathered to swap gossip, ensure our place within the group and talk endlessly about who pashed who at the last party. As the comic I had access to all the steps; but only if my material was good. I got to float around with the popular girls because I was funny. But I wanted something that would guarantee my position, not just give me access. I had to be like these girls or have something they envied. I didn't want to end up dancing in the middle on my own again. It was on the steps of the amphitheatre that I learnt how to diet and binge, control my life by controlling my body, ignore my hunger and curb my appetite.

I noticed other girls who did not qualify through looks, or contacts, or wealth vie for their position with good grades or daring behaviour like smoking in the toilets, short uniforms or handing out Daddy's alcohol.

All the time we were told it was our minds that mattered, our grades, our sporting achievements (and the ability of our parents to pay the fees on time) but we knew it was about which boy you dated, what your father did, which designer you wore, how long your legs were, how blonde your hair was, how svelte your waist and how toned your quads. We knew it because we talked about it every lunch hour.

On school excursions Andrea Beckett and I would steal gargantuan bars of chocolate from the freeway motor stop and inhale them in the back of the bus. The next stop was spent by the side of the road, fingers down the back of the throat, watching the brown muck come back up. We couldn't devour chocolate and keep our position in the amphitheatre so we binged and purged rather than lose our place.

Secretly I envied the girls in our form who did devour the chocolate and didn't care about a place on the amphitheatre steps. But they were probably bingeing while I was purging, and for the same reason, because they just wanted to fit in and didn't know how to do it. Other girls spent more time with their textbooks, or played netball, tennis and hockey, or sniffed Liquid Paper and ate Perkins Paste. All because they wanted to fit in and couldn't or because they did fit in and were scared that one day they wouldn't.

A tendency to compare myself to others, a need for constant attention and the shame I felt about my body made me a running candidate for an eating disorder. It could have been a drug habit if the combination had been skewed slightly differently, or a penchant for alcohol or gambling or some other destructive behaviour to fill in the blank.

All this time on the amphitheatre steps I hovered between a size twelve and fourteen. At least that's what I remember. My memory is so strongly influenced by my body image of the time that I can't be sure what my real size was. I believed I was a fourteen and wanted to be an eight. For all I know I could have been a size ten or a twelve. Either way I was not enormous but I was bigger than the average and aware of it every day. I had stopped growing taller and had watched as girls who were starting puberty sprouted over me.

The rules of high-school girl behaviour changed when sexual competition came into play. If I ventured into schoolboy train-station flirting I thought I was going to be found out, that they would see that the Fat Funny Girl was just plain fat and she put the funny on. I was popular, I was not fat, I did well at school but I always felt I was one joke away from the 'out crowd'. Instinctively I knew I had better enter the sexual arena or lose my position in the 'in crowd' and end up alone at the bottom of the steps at lunchtime.

So on those occasions when I ventured forth into unknown testosterone territory I was loud, I was funny, and hoped my mouth would keep the attention away from my body. The third shelf of the Westinghouse was my Saturday night pashing partner. It had to be because if I did go to the party and pash a boy then how could I trust myself to stop? I did not stop at the third shelf but went on to devour the fourth and fifth, so why would boys be any different? Better to stay home than take the risk, be rejected or become a slut.

By this stage my bingeing had developed from stealing cupcakes from the Harrison house to buying custard tarts and a handful of Redskins at the corner store to stuffing down still-frozen food from my mother's fridge. My school days were spent dreaming of the food I would eat on my way home, always with my hat pulled down low over my head lest someone see me eating. I did not want anyone to make the connection between the food in my hand at the bus stop and the size of my thighs. My bingeing had come out of my bedroom and into the rest of my life.

THINDARELLA

AT FIFTEEN I WAS KEEN to accumulate Brownie points for my school report and volunteered for community service. I was assigned a respectable old people's home where BMW-driving professionals kept their aged parents from spending any more of their inheritance.

Most of the occupants lived alone in one-roomed apartments with the smell of lollies and old age in the air. Like me, they had a sweet tooth and they liked nothing more than to sit with a box of Terry's jellies and a cup of tea and have a good chat about their grandchildren. As most of my school day was spent devising ways to binge on the way home despite my empty wallet I was usually in a pre-binge frenzy by the time I reached the nursing home.

If I had not had such an aversion to sugared jelly fruits I daresay I would have whipped the orange gelatin from between their dentures, but even I had certain lines I was not willing to cross. So instead I stole their dinners from the trolleys and binged on puréed roasts and trifles. It could have been my own grandmother I was stealing from, had she not been safely six foot under.

With entrepreneurial inventiveness, I went to great lengths to find food or money for food. In Year Nine I stumbled upon the brilliant idea of selling chocolate for charity. My charity. I made trays of caramel fudge bars dipped in rice bubbles and chocolate and sold them to my schoolmates, insisting the money would go to the Spastic Centre. Instead the proceeds would go into my hip pocket and fund the fish and chips, cream horns and chocolate eclairs at the end of the day. I sold food under false pretences to make money to buy the food I really wanted.

Each year our school held a professional chocolate drive where we would dutifully purchase boxes of ten bars of chocolate and sell them to our family and neighbours for the school charity. This was a binger's heaven as girls' unattended lockers burst at the seams with chocolate-coated almonds and rich bars big enough to break teeth. I waited until class started before I raided the empty form rooms for my bounty. The girls would have to make up the value of the bars lost to my hunger.

Like bulimics and compulsive eaters around the world I never binged in front of anyone. I was careful to ensure the coast was clear when I stole from the old people and the girls in the forms below. On the outside I was happy, fun-loving and polite to teachers. This ensured that no one would suspect me should any food go missing.

There was nothing I would not do in the throes of a binge. I would have stolen bread from the Bosnians if I had to, but I made do with geriatric pensioners and spastics. Any moral fibre I had was lost in the midst of a binge cycle. The lower I sank, the bigger the binge; the bigger the binge, the lower I sank. The lower I sank the deeper the despair, the more aggressive the self-loathing, the bigger the binge.

When Katrina Rowland came to school eight kilos lighter after two weeks of eating eggs, grapefruit and boiled chicken on the Scarsdale Diet, I thought I had found the quick answer to beauty and popularity. If boys were interested in me like they were in Katrina, then my position in the group would be secure, so long as I controlled my appetite. If I controlled what went into my body then I could control a kiss, have the boys, and accept the invites. Dieting could get rid of my curves for good, I thought.

Like generations of women before me, I threw myself into dieting like a nun into religion. I had witnessed what it could do for Katrina and I wanted it to do the same for me. Change my body, change my shape and change my place on the steps of the amphitheatre. I prostrated myself before Dr Scarsdale, Jenny Craig, Jane Fonda and twenty-five thousand other gurus of self-denial with a video to flog. The Israeli Army Diet became my daily regime. I was a Christian girl on the North Shore of Sydney experimenting with diets designed to beat Syrians in the desert and I felt I was winning the fight. I signed up for Gloria Marshall and wore dark glasses and a trench coat for my weekly visits after school.

I was driven in my dieting. Eyes glazed from lack of nutrients, mind numb, I gladly tried anything to get my diet fix. The Russian Princess In Flight Diet consisted of the bark of two trees and a potato. I wrapped the potato in bark and devoured the lot in one sitting, then found out it was supposed to last me a week. I lost my dignity as I crouched over the toilet bowl, with an empty bottle of Lose Ten Stone in a Day at my feet. I counted calories, inches, millimetres, centimetres, fatometres, kilos, pounds, stone, ounces, grams and fibre density.

I paid a doctor in a white coat the equivalent of my private school fees to rid me of my childhood fat. He prescribed strawberries and rockmelon five times a day and measured my fat rolls with a pair of pliers. When I discovered the 275 calorie count of Mars Bars I went on my own 'Three Mars A Day (and nothing else) Makes You Taut, Best, Hooray' diet, losing more than five kilos on 825 calories per day. My skin looked like shit but boy, my stomach was flat. Think I'm joking?

Whenever a diet didn't work, as it inevitably wouldn't,

when I broke my resolve and found myself with my head in the fridge I would bargain with myself and my body. How many justifications for weight gain does a girl need? It's the fluid retention. I'm about to get my period. My feet have swollen in the heat so it stands to reason my thighs have done the same. These jeans are fresh out of the wash and they need to stretch. Bugger it, I'm fat and I need to go on a diet. I have four weeks till the school formal. I can start my diet on Sunday. Okay, I'll start Monday, it's the beginning of the week officially anyway. When I finally decided on a start date I would ship in the necessary supplies, carrots, celery, soup, crackers, fruit, never realising it was a diet that got me fat in the first place.

As I lost weight, all the girls wanted to know my secret, to join my club, and I handed out dieting advice each day at noon. 'Eat nothing with flavour, weigh yourself at the same time every day, best in the morning, don't mix protein with carbs, carbs with fibre, fibre with water, potatoes and oranges, or fun with food.' I pounded, prodded, pushed, poked, puked my body into perfection and got high when I felt my boobs disappearing.

I was still invited to the parties, and this time I went, keeping my mouth closed so no food could get in and no appetite could get out. At one such party I discovered the ultimate diet that worked. I fell in lurve.

Falling in love – the ultimate appetite suppressant. With each kiss with my new beau I lost a kilo. I did not want my new boyfriend discarding me because I was fat.

Food sat unopened in my fridge as I sat by the phone in anticipation of his call. A fifteen-year-old Prince Charming rescued me from my appetite and I found power in my slim-lined body. Dieting got me the body, the body got me the boy and the boy got me the seat next to the cool chicks in maths class. My new body and my new boy had all the girls talking and I rested on my bones in the limelight. I dropped him when he went a step further than pashing, petrified that his fingers down my knickers would unleash the insatiable appetite I fought so hard to control.

The rules of virginity at an all-girls school are complex and must be adhered to. Don't lose your virginity before Year Eleven, and if you do don't tell anyone. Always lose your virginity to a boy you have been dating for at least three months. Stay with him until final year exams and if you do break up don't sleep with anyone else. One sexual penetratory partner per girl; any more and you're easy – save the multiple partners for university. If you lose your virginity too early the girls will call you a slut; if you lose it too late the boys will say you are frigid. Move with the pack and stay in the middle, don't steal other girls' boyfriends unless you want to be considered easy. When your friends ask say you have done 'everything but' even if you have yet to hit second base or have already scored a home run.

At seventeen, it was officially time for me to lose my virginity. In my final year of school I fell in love, and right on target, three months later, gave my body away to 'him'. Overnight we became sex gods.

I was a child in an adult's playground, tantalising my boyfriend and believing that if he wanted my body then he wanted me. I did not mind this boy touching my body or seeing me naked as long as I was thin, but as my sexual drive was released I began to eat to swallow the conflicting feelings I had towards my body. I put on a couple of kilos at the most but I started to turn the light off during our love-making and sneak to the bathroom with the sheet wrapped around me. Eventually there came the day where my body was no longer enough and he finished the relationship for good, breaking my heart over the phone.

For two weeks I lived off nothing but crumbs, punishing my body for letting me down. I got off on the weight loss and introduced early morning bike rides and late evening aerobics into my life. I said no to my mother's offer of cream buns, Tim Tams and chocolate Yogos. I watched her eat them instead and I felt saintly by comparison. I stayed firm and in control and monitored every morsel that entered my mouth. 'He'll want me now,' I thought as I cried myself to sleep each night. My body regressed in years as my breasts and hips disappeared. In the same way I had eaten to hide my sexuality I was now starving to do the same.

I could not control my ex-boyfriend's love for me and I could not control my final year exams so I controlled my body instead. Anorexia became a lifestyle decision. When my hunger raised its head I pushed it back down. If it took over I threw it back up into the porcelain bowl. I stripped my innards with laxatives and prayed for food poisoning so I could lose weight. At one point, I enticed my ex-boyfriend back into my bed. Where once there'd been curves there were angles and I felt like a minor in a porn movie. But my thin body wasn't enough to keep him under my covers. He said he wanted my flesh back but I knew it was my flesh that had deceived me and was determined not to let it return.

I was anorexic but in true anorexic style I denied it emphatically. I knew no one could possibly exist on the minuscule amount of food I was eating and I knew that a bike ride before school followed by an aerobics session and weights workout after school was not normal teenage behaviour. Girls in my year had been anorexic before me. Some had been admitted into hospital; others slipped quietly out of the school. But I never thought that it would happen to me.

The control and the power I had over my hunger and my body gave me a high. For weeks on end I lived off the rush of knowing I was losing weight and could lose more. The day I broke the fifty kilo mark on the bathroom scales I used daily was a major highlight in my anorexic life. I had done it, I had gotten below the magic fifty; now if I could only hit forty five. I wish I was forty-five, I wish I was forty-five, I wish I was forty-five.

My mother had long ago given up trying to control her rebellious third child and knew there was no point in trying to get me to eat. Every time she offered me food I resisted, answering with a firm 'no'. She took to leaving open packets of chocolate biscuits out on the kitchen counter for when I got home but these were no match for my rigid control.

The more attention I got the more I thrived. Teachers pulled me aside for quiet chats about my body, asking me if the pressure of the final year exams was too much. I smiled sweetly and told them they had nothing to worry about. The extra fabric of my now over-large uniform made me feel fantastic. Look at all this extra room, I can feel my bones brushing against the metres of fabric. How can I not have felt this before, it's pure magic.

I flaunted my anorexic body in the beer garden on Thursday nights, in a hipster skirt with midriff top. The boys touched my waist and I laughed like they do in the movies and felt powerful.

Some anorexics flaunt their body for The Gaze. Look at me, look at me, look how much I am suffering. Look how my ribs stick out, bet yours don't do that. My bikini bottom stretched taut across my hip bones, leaving me with a full view of the mound of my pubic hair when I lay on my back. That gave me more pleasure than I could imagine.

Fifty-five kilos, forty-nine kilos, forty-eight, forty-seven, forty-six and counting. I couldn't keep it up and in panic began purging what little I did eat. On schoolies' week after my final year exams I ate a packet of Twisties, then immediately stuck my fingers down my throat and choked as orange-coloured spit fell into the bowl. I never mastered the art of self-induced vomiting and moved on to laxatives and Ipecac syrup when the need to purge took hold. This, combined with constant exercise, ensured I remained underweight around the fifty-kilo mark for the first year out of high school. No longer anorexic, for I was eating, I tottered on the fence between anorexia and bulimia.

Starving myself and purging whenever I ate: bulimarexic.

I returned to my anorexic ways many times later in my life, starving myself till my bones pushed through my skin whenever I broke up with a boyfriend. But it was never the same. I had to work harder each time. Remember that one magical diet that worked? The diet when you lost all that weight and got into those Barbie-sized jeans. We remember that diet with pride and measure all other diets by it. We often try to return to that diet and to those pre-shrunk jeans but it never works in the same way again. After reaching forty-six kilos I spent a good part of the rest of my life believing 'I have got to get back there'. I never did. I got close but age, a damaged metabolism and a desire to binge prevented me.

I never entered hospital, although I am sure there are those who felt I should have. At Christmas time I exhibited my thin body in a bikini and small T-shirt as I opened my presents, trying to piss off my sisters: look how much skinnier I am than you. When offered food I would decline, saying I had put on weight and was on a diet to get rid of my fat thighs. Whoever was in earshot would roll their eyes and sigh. I had turned into one of those annoying stick figure girls who always complained in loud voices 'I am so fat' just so everyone else can deny it.

When I graduated from school I walked a tightrope with food, balancing hot dogs with carrot sticks, ice-cream with crackers, careful not to fall off the thin rope into the fat precipice below. Men wanted me, women envied me and I despised my uncontrollable body and myself. Forty-six, forty-seven, forty-nine and counting. All that starvation had set me up for a binge; the more I starved, the bigger the binge when it inevitably happened.

As a teenager just out of school I worked as a banquet waitress at an international hotel, serving high flyers their quail and blancmange. I became best friends with the pastry chef (I knew which side my freshly baked bread was buttered). Each evening at the end of service the dessert trolley had to be returned to the pastry kitchen one floor above. Many a minute was spent in the service lift as I stopped the elevator between floors and gorged on all three trays of the trolley. Then I'd wipe my mouth clean of cream, custard and crumbs, restart the lift and nonchalantly shuffle into the pastry kitchen pushing a somewhat lighter dessert trolley. It never took long and no one knew.

My first real job after school was as an office junior at an advertising firm. I was given the responsibility of balancing the petty cash each month. I had the only key to the petty cash tin in the third drawer down. So when a binge hit I thought nothing of dipping into the tin to fund my insatiable hunger. Then I would fill the tin with generic receipts found in my mother's wallet in an effort to balance the bottom line every month.

Should the urge to binge hit me on a weekend when my bank balance happened to be low I could always wander the aisles of Woolworths, opening chocolate bars, soy snacks and cookie boxes as I went. A trail of empty packets was left in my wake and I walked out empty-handed with a full stomach and no payment necessary.

The petty larceny my bingeing forced me into served to fuel my self-disgust further. As the binge subsided it wasn't just my thighs I lamented. I hated myself not only for my lack of control but for my blatant disrespect for my 'nice' upbringing.

During my second year out of school I was working for a design team who were Australia's darlings of the fashion scene. I was employed to manage their clothing store. I was still a petite size eight and delighted in parading the shop floor in their latest range. In the first few months I made record sales, increasing their revenue and my commission with vigour. Nights after work were filled with tequila races at the local pub where I enjoyed minor celebrity status among the fashion wannabes. Predictably, I began to get bored. Selling disposable fashion to Sydney's hip young crowd did not provide me with much mental stimulation. Neither did the gourmet cafés next door with who I was on first name terms.

Crumbed wiener schnitzel smothered in mayonnaise, avocado, Swiss cheese and tomato and hemmed in by two slabs of baguette became my focus. I dreamt about the honey-crumbed meat on my way to work each morning. By midday I was cramming it into my mouth and washing it down with chocolate and Cheezels. Inexhaustible in my hunger, I did not know how to stop and often attempted to purge at the end of the day long after the food had already settled on my thighs.

Not surprisingly, with this excess came an increase in weight. Size eight became size ten and size ten eventually became size twelve. With their tendency to create clothes for the under-weight midget, my fashion designer employers stopped their range at a size twelve (the average size of an Australian woman is a size fourteen). There were still clothes for me to wear but they were limited by my continuous gorging behaviour. Sales were right on target but I was bored with my life.

One of the designers spoke to me one day about the increase in my size. No doubt she felt my body was her property and with the deed of ownership came the right to renovate. She told me I must lose weight or lose my job. Something about image for the label. In her own way she was trying to set a limit on me and I rebelled. I was horrified that she had pointed out my excess and brought the consequences of it into the light.

I declined their delightful suggestion that I lose weight and handed in my resignation. It never occurred to me to suggest they make larger sizes but then it never occurred to them either. My binge eating and drinking increased as I said 'fuck you' with every mouthful. 'Fuck you' became 'fuck me' as I hid from the world behind my fat.

My mouth did the talking, the seducing and the eating. I spent my first two years out of high school hiding my bingeing from my various employers. Weekends were spent marinated in vodka in someone else's bed, then devouring the fridge shelf upon my return home. My struggle with myself as a child in this grown-up world landed me in bedrooms with boys who promised me love for at least the night. I refused to look at my body and gave it away time and time again. When food wouldn't do it for me, a one-night stand would. 'Please take my body away from me', I would cry silently as he reached a climax. Then I'd sniffle in the back of the cab home, ordering the driver into the fast food drive-through: 'ah wanna urger iv aaah lot'.

I hated my body because it let me down. It had caused me humiliation at my ballet class, it had not kept my first boyfriend in my bed and now it had cost me my job. Every girl gets dumped by her first boyfriend at some time, we're all humiliated when we are young and can't do something, and losing a job the second year out of school is no great tragedy. But by this stage I was so used to blaming my body for everything from early puberty on that it was second nature to blame it some more.

I became unhinged when my school yard Prince Charming did not save me and I believed if I got thin then he would. I became thin and when I remained unsaved after school I went in search of other boys who could come to my rescue. Fat, food and love were so intertwined that I mistook one for the other and believed I could control the love I did or did not receive simply by changing the size of my body.

I had begun to confuse sex with love and food with sex. My body could provide sex for me when I wanted love and then food could fill the gaping hole left the next morning. If I could not get sex or love then I could always stay in with a family block of Cadburys. My sinewy thighs were forever tensed, ready to pounce on the first male who looked my way. When I was thin I could discard him (there would always be another), when I thought I was fat I clung on to him tightly in fear he would get away.

I did not expect them all to ring like they'd promised although I secretly hoped they would. I placed my life in danger by trusting strangers time and time again. This only happened when I was thin. When I was fat I dared not venture forth for fear of rejection. Everybody likes the funny fat girl until she wants to sleep with you. I used sex as a form of purging, bingeing on alcohol at the bar, purging with sex in the bedroom.

Part of me believed the man would save me from my body and in turn myself. In order to get Prince Charming I had to be Thindarella. But when I became Thindarella Prince Charming never called. At almost nineteen years of age I point-blank refused to acknowledge my body as that of a woman. I was sucking my thumb as I passed out in an alcoholic stupor.

Thus began the Cycle of Self-Loathing: I hate myself for having one-night stands, I have sex to get rid of the hate, I hate myself for having one-night stands. I hate myself for eating, I eat to get rid of the hate, I hate myself for eating. I would alternate one-night stands with shopping, shopping with eating, eating with drinking; they all kept me on the Cycle of Self-Loathing and enabled me to blame the things that allowed me to remain on the loop. I blamed my body for the one-night stands, for without it I would not get sex; I blamed my appetite for my eating, for without it I would not eat; I blamed my credit card for my shopping, for without it I could not shop; I blamed my body for my drinking, for without it I did not get free drinks.

I was still living at home with my parents and hiding my destructive behaviour. Beneath my bed the pile of empty laxative packets, food wrappers and nightclub match boxes built up. My mother knew not to venture inside. I had a separate bathroom so my parents did not hear my midnight retching and laxative release.

When I lost weight I felt responsible for men's advances towards me; after all, it was my body that made them want me. How could I say no when it was my flesh that got me into this position in the first place? I felt obliged to show some interest, to 'put out'. I didn't want to be called a prick teaser so I chose to behave like a slut.

As relationships started I was forever throwing my body away. Here, you take responsibility for it; I don't want it. I'd fake orgasms, hoping it would get the sexual act over and done with so I did not have to remain in my body or accept the grown-up act I was engaging in. My body was evil (or so I thought) and would soon cause my downfall with devastating consequences.

A POUND OF FLESH

One Sunday night in Sydney, aged 19, I was raped.

Out on the town, I was coated in an alcoholic glaze with the beat of Duran Duran leading my dancing feet on. My best friend left me at the club to go home early, happy in the knowledge that I was safe from harm with the male family friend she had left in charge. He bought me drinks and told me he would make sure I got home safely. Sweet of him, I thought.

Two hours later he suggested we move on to a party he had been invited to in a neighbouring suburb. I was happy when he suggested a detour to pick up champagne from his home. I was not so happy when he locked the front door behind us as we went in. I was alarmed when he pulled my hair tight, and whispered close to my ear that we were going to have sex together. He was unhappy when I refused and unhappier still when I tried to leave. He showed me his gun collection and I was terrified. Then he pushed me outside to my car, where he forced me to perform oral sex before raping me on the bonnet.

I left my body inside his house with the gun collection. I hovered above the figures on the bonnet of my car. This can't be happening, I thought, this can't be happening, this can't be happening. The bruises on my back showed otherwise.

He discarded me mid-rape when I turned the power trip around and offered my body for him to play. 'What would you like me to do now?' I asked and he immediately lost his erection and threw me aside. At that life-saving moment, in his eyes I had become a willing party and the excitement was gone. I drove home as the sun rose on the new day, leaving myself behind.

I thought I deserved it. I thought I deserved it because I was thin. I believed my body had let me down. If I had been fat and unattractive this never would have happened. I wanted to slice my flesh off with sharp knives. Instead, paralysed by fear and self-loathing, I began to eat.

Instinctively I knew I could not report the attack. A blood test would reveal my alcohol intake. The impact of the welts and bruises would fade to nothing in a court of law if they started dragging my one-night stands in. I asked myself if I had been a willing party when I tried to save myself and offered myself to him mid-rape. That life-saving instinct would have the lawyers calling me a whore.

Two weeks after being raped I was at a nightclub and saw the same man. I did not attack him. I did not run. I did not scream or cry. Instead, I spoke to him as if nothing had happened.

He offered me drugs, Quaaludes, he said. The next eight hours were then cut from my life's reel. I have no recollection of what happened. I had been given Rohypnol. He did not rape me this time. Instead a friend who was with me saved me from my own self-destruction and gave me a couch to pass out on.

I was so used to giving my body away that when a man did take it without my permission I went back to him to ask him to take it again. I was so desperate to be rid of the body that was always getting in my way that I was willing to accept drugs from a man who had raped me only weeks before. I was so convinced that I had asked for what happened, that I was more concerned as to how he felt about me than how I felt about myself.

The rape rendered me powerless, silent, speechless. I told only one friend of my plight, revealing the deep, black marks down my spine. She told me to keep quiet. I didn't need encouraging. I had shut myself up in his room that night and hadn't heard from myself since.

If I was determined to remain a child before the rape then I became driven in my irrational, childish behaviour after. The thin me was left behind as I gorged on schnitzel, avocado, chocolate and cake. I looked at my body with loathing and disgust, stooping to bin-raiding to eat myself away. My destructive behaviour increased as I shopped with abandon, drank myself stupid, snorted strangers' cocaine and drove under the influence.

The refusal to acknowledge my body as a grown woman, the desire to remain childlike in an anorexic frame, the inability to say no to the men who groped me and the assault on my body by another person had cost me dearly. If I was forever behaving like a child I was now becoming a victim of child abuse at my own hands. My bulimia increased and I started mistreating laxatives on a more regular basis.

I remained a child for years after that night on the bonnet of my car. I juggled one-night stands with binge eating and vomiting or exercising excessively and I ran up unpayable debts. I refused to acknowledge what was going on.

At twenty-one I was accepted into Drama School. I got the dream I had wanted: three years in full-time acting school. Only I did not know what to do with it. I was terrified I would have to reveal my thighs in movement class and petrified the teachers would see through my 'act' and loathe me as much as I did. I wrote to the school and declined.

London looked like a fabulous option. If I travelled fast enough and far enough then I could leave the rape and my body behind. I took to my newfound plan to improve my life with travel the way I took to dieting, believing this journey would change everything. I bought into the glamorous image of exotic locations, smiling faces, holiday romances and espressos on the piazza. Homesickness, lack of funds and stolen backpacks did not come into the equation.

If I went to England then I could reinvent myself. I could become anyone but me because no one knew me over there. I planned to spend a year but I knew I might not return. So I cleaned up the wrappers under my bed, booked my ticket and prepared for my overseas sojourn. I told myself I was still pursuing my dream, and I applied for a four-week drama summer school in London and was accepted.

My father arranged for a supplementary Visa card from his account to be used in emergencies. He filled out the appropriate form and left it for me to sign. In the space provided for credit limit he had written $4000. Not happy with what I saw as a moderate limit, I increased it by $2000 before mailing it in. Now I had it all, overseas travel and a credit card to make those postcard scenes come true.

Once I got overseas I created 'emergencies' daily and used the card, swiping it for clothes, books, records, dinners. Homesick? Go shopping. I was bingeing with my credit card with a vengeance. At the depths of my binge-eating depression I was living in a council squat in London and dining at all the best restaurants, thanks to Dad. I reached the $6000 limit on my credit card and pushed right through it, almost tripling it in the process. No one was going to restrict me – no bank, no father, no employers. I ate and spent, ate and spent, ate and spent and put on weight. When my Visa card was no longer accepted I moved on to American Express with its limitless seduction.

Finally my parents cancelled my cards. I ate non-stop for

two weeks, using food as a temper tantrum. Piling on kilos to add to the store I had already dumped onto my body. I was now a size sixteen. Again I was saying fuck you, fuck you, fuck you as I reached for another Marks & Spencers Viennese shortbread. I didn't know it at the time but it wasn't my parents I was fucking, it was me.

I travelled to Europe and left behind my excessive London persona that had replaced my excessive Sydney persona. I attempted to re-invent myself in the only way I knew how – dieting.

A year after leaving home I had starved my way around Europe and Canada and was back in London half the size I was when I left Australia. I was not ready to return home to the persona I loathed. I was still waiting for my exotic life to fire up in England. I cashed in my return ticket and got a job managing a restaurant where my property key afforded me open access to binge food twenty-four hours a day. Laxatives and gym memberships ensured my bingeing went undetected on my body.

And that's where I met Sebastian. He was an English toff of the Hugh Grant variety in a front-row forward frame. Charming Sebastian with an apartment from Daddy, an estate in the country; heir to a fortune. Seduced by his crooning voice, his millionaire manners and a dozen red roses, I agreed to move into his spare room as a fifty-pounds-a-week tenant and then moved into his bed for nothing.

Ours was a love/hate relationship. The common denominator was that we both hated ourselves. My self-hate manifested in early morning binges and late night purges; his in drinking benders. I thought he could save me from my bulimia, my compulsive spending and my memories of being raped but living with him was not enough to stop me from doubling over in the toilet three times a day.

It was easy to hide my bulimia from Sebastian. When he left for work in the morning I went to the local store to stock up on pastries and doughnuts. By the time my post-binge laxatives were taking effect he was still an hour away from returning home. As he returned I went off to work the night shift at a restaurant and he began his drinking. We were a tag team of self-destructive behaviour. If he was aware of my disordered eating he never made comment and I kept silent about his alcoholic mood swings: if you don't point out my alcoholism I won't mention your bulimia.

When he shouted alcoholic abuse at me I did not flinch. He was only voicing what I already said to myself each day. When he locked me out of the house I knew I deserved it for I would have locked myself out too. When he asked me to wear twinsets and pearls I knew he was trying to turn me into something I wasn't and I secretly thanked him for he could see I was not worthy as I was.

I had the life: an apartment in London with a well-bred millionaire, trips to the country for croquet on weekends and fine dining in London during the week. He told me he would marry me, and I met his family, but that still was not enough to stop me spending money I did not have on clothes I never wore and food I always ate. I fell pregnant to him and he said he wanted to keep the baby, but that too was not enough to stop me or him from drinking the bar dry each Saturday night. I was a child, not a woman, and a child cannot give birth to a child so I had an abortion and did not blink.

Fifteen months into our relationship when he chose another woman to share his bed I stopped eating. I was back at school, seventeen again, ditched by the man I gave my virginity to. My body had not been enough to keep this one either, so I retreated into starvation. If my butt gets smaller then he will want me; if my stomach is flat then he'll need me; if my upper arms are toned then he will marry me; if he marries me then he will save me. I returned to my anorexic behaviour of old, refused to eat and joined the gym. The kilos dropped off me.

When he showed up at my place of work four weeks after our break-up I thought he had come to his senses and was there to lament his loss. Instead he told me he was engaged to his new floozy and invited me to the wedding, at one stage suggesting I host the kitchen tea! Three days after this news had sunk in I arranged to meet him in the pub to pick up mail for me that had been sent to his house. When I arrived he was there with his fiancée.

This is where I fantasised about throwing a pint of beer in his and her face and ripping his wandering dick out of his pants while declaring to the pub he had given me genital warts. Instead I smiled sweetly and accepted her offer of a gin and tonic. Two drinks later I agreed to go to dinner with the man who had broken my heart and the woman who had moved into my bed. I was so terrified they wouldn't like me that I could not set limits on their or my behaviour. I returned to the man who dealt out the abuse, just as I did when I was ninetten. I hated myself afterwards and tried to retain some dignity by leaving dinner halfway through and telling the fiancée that she was a fool – only it wasn't her face that was red.

I was in London, dumped by my boyfriend and living in hell. My body was tiny and gym workouts twice a day ensured it remained that way. I was working as a waitress in one of the best kitchens in England. Any resolve to stop bingeing melted when I walked through the kitchen door and prepared for my shift. My sweet tooth was soothed daily by the contents of the dessert fridge. I spent my working day writing out fake orders (which never made it to the cash register) for empty tables who requested chocolate fudge brownies, sticky date pudding and lemon tarts by the dozen. I would stash my loot in a cupboard in the bread corner where I could swallow entire trays of fudge brownies while slicing bread, my back to the restaurant and my binge undetected. Of course he left me, the bastard; I hate him, I hate me, I am a fat pig.

Then one day a solid padlock stood between me and the bread and butter pudding. I had thought the dessert fridge was my secret passion. It held more than lemon tart encased in sweet pastry, more than sticky toffee pudding backstroking in syrup, more than chocolate fudge brownies to melt the resolve. It held the glue to my life. I was caught out; the fat police had slipped in overnight and locked in the evidence. I was mortified. In a restaurant catering for more than 200 people per night and a kitchen heaving with activity I had thought my penchant for slabs of sugar had gone undetected. What's a missing chocolate mud cake or five between friends? I could only hope they hadn't lifted my fingerprints from the brownies or checked dental records against the lemon tart.

Undeterred, I soon discovered where they kept the key and waited until after-hours to do my foraging. Other times I paced, watching for tables that left any dessert on the plate. As soon as the customer rested their fork on the plate and almost before they had pushed their finished (but half-eaten) dessert away, I pounced and cleared the table of dirty dishes before they had a chance to change their mind and take another bite. Then I would make a beeline for the trusty bread corner where I dropped off the half-eaten pudding before clearing the rest in the kitchen and nipping back to the bread corner for another quick fix.

When I worked days, the handover from the breakfast shift to the day shift included baskets of croissants and danishes left over from breakfasting tourists. I would count the minutes down to close of breakfast service when I could whisk away the basket into the staff room and shove two, three, four at a time into my gullet. The rest of the shift was then spent complaining about my elephant arms and pinching my own arse.

When there were no croissants left over I circled the dessert fridge again and ate calves' liver and sausages from customers' luncheon plates. I felt like a dog, a mangy stray starving mutt, scavenging the bins in the side alley. I had no thought for hygiene and no self-respect.

As many a food junkie can tell you, we flock to industries obsessed with food. I spent years working as a waitress in all manner of restaurants, supplementing my calorific income with hours at the gym and making best friends with Senokot laxatives.

You wouldn't believe me if I said I was unaware of my behaviour, and neither would I. I knew I was bulimic; there was enough press coverage about Princess Diana to know that we shared the same compulsive toilet behaviour. It had to be bulimia; what person in their right mind would spend half their pay on food and the other half on laxatives? But knowing it and admitting it were two different matters.

After my break up with Sebastian my sternum began to reappear. This filled me with great pride. I had returned to my bulimarexic behaviour and it was working.

My parents arrived in London six months after Sebastian and I had broken up to find an even skinnier version of the daughter they had last seen two years before. Lord knows what they thought of this gym-junkie waif who one day hid behind oversized jumpers and the next appeared in hip-hugging lycra.

I told them one day in a restaurant in Soho. I just came right out and said it. 'Mum, Dad, I am bulimic.'

My father sat stunned. My mother looked around the room, avoiding my eyes, as she said, 'Don't you think I have known that?' Then my father joined in. 'I thought you were stronger than that.'

Mum, why did you not stop me? But how could she have stopped me when I slammed the door in her face?

Dad, I am strong. Look at me, Dad. I am telling you something really really hard for me to say. That takes strength, Dad.

My father took action. He's a businessman and can take care of things if they are tangible. Now I had given my behaviour a name he could tackle it. He went in search of rehab units and doctors who specialise in eating disorders. Doctors I never saw and rehab units I never visited. I had confessed my behaviour but was still not prepared to let go of a lifetime habit.

My mother hugged me tight at the airport when they left to go home.

After three more months in London, my father called me from Sydney and asked me what I wanted to do. I decided to go home. I booked a return ticket because I believed I could tackle this in a couple of months and run back to London. Seven years later I still have not made it back.

So I returned home to Australia, a self-confessed late twenties bulimarexic in what looked like a ten-year-old's body, still on the Cycle of Self-Loathing.

WHAT GOES DOWN MUST COME BACK UP AGAIN

THE TROUBLE WITH LAXATIVES is that you can't control when you're going to shit. They take hours to take effect and when they do you had better pray you are within spitting distance of a bucket, a bin, a sandpit, or the infants' aisle of your local chemist.

Ipecac syrup is one of the alternatives to laxatives available to the bulimic. It is a liquid vomit-inducer available across the counter of your neighbourhood pharmacy. Ipecac is a clean, controlled technique that rids the body of the five hot dogs, three-and-a-quarter banana milkshakes, two frozen cheesecakes and one White Wings packet cake mix devoured raw half an hour earlier. Simply fill a teaspoon with the sticky nectar, take a breath, swallow and wait.

Fifteen minutes later the body will start to sweat, cramp and convulse. The entire contents of your stomach will then project themselves across the space in front of you, leaving you empty, bare and prepared for the next binge (after you've cleaned up).

I have never been able to vomit without chemical assistance. Even with my arm half-way down my throat the contents of my stomach refused to budge. Shoving a toothbrush down my throat did not work, twelve litres of mustard-spiked water gave me heartburn and milk mixed with orange juice made me feel ill but I still did not vomit.

With a stomach of cast iron I could easily down enough food to save a small starving nation in one single sitting. Once downed, it had nowhere to go but my thighs.

Of course, the inability to vomit can be a major obstacle to bulimia.

For the uninitiated a binge is defined by its secret nature. If a binge is done in full view of people then it is not a binge; it is simply gluttony. The clandestine nature of bingeing keeps the binge cycle alive. Binge in private, purge in private, starve in public. I was the size of a sparrow with a public appetite to match but as soon as the front door closed behind me I had the appetite of a lion.

My bingeing did not discriminate. It always left me in a state of self-degradation and there were times that it affected the lives of others. It is one thing to damage myself and another to damage others in the process. My bingeing sometimes meant others went hungry, but that was not my concern. I stole sandwiches, dinners, bread and money but stealing wasn't the problem; where I ate my stash was. I ate it in private, in secret, alone and terrified of being caught. If I was caught out then I would have to acknowledge what I was doing and at times what I was doing was too gross for me to look at.

I have been known to devour two tubs of Baskin and Robbins Pralines 'n' Cream in one sitting, washing it down with a block of vintage cheddar, a six pack of coconut biscuits, a family-sized chicken-and-leek pie and a frozen Sara Lee cake.

There is no such thing as a dumb bulimic. The intelligence required to prevent detection ensures that dumb bulimics don't last long. A studious binger will choose her binge moments with care, will think nothing of driving twenty kilometres to shop at a Woolworths undetected and she never leaves home without dark glasses and a wig in the car as binge backup.

A dumb binger creates a trail of wrappers as evidence in her path, leaves the front door unlocked and has an account at the local supermarket in her own name.

Binge eating skills can take a number of years to perfect. I learnt to drive with one hand while unwrapping fast food with the other and diverting glances from surrounding motorists. I knew where to hide the wrappers in my car, how to binge when broke, which cakes can be eaten frozen and how to inhale a packet of Tim Tams while on the way to work without ruining my lipstick.

It's an exhausting process, binge eating. The professional binger needs stamina and tenacity and an ability to keep one ear out for approaching friends, relatives and strangers. One never knows when the binge is going to drop by. Sometimes it taps you on the shoulder when you wake up in the morning and other times it may wait until the mid-afternoon marketing meeting to raise its seductive head. Many a binger has spent hours planning a post-work binge when she should have been planning the budget for the next financial quarter.

Binges are private rituals and must be done in secret with the fridge light off. If any light shines on the binge process then the binger may cotton on to what she is doing and stop, and that doesn't make for a good bulimic. Eyes wide shut in denial is the name of the binge eating game. I accepted my mission time and time again, sometimes hurting other people, sometimes, not but always, degrading myself in the process.

When I lived at home with my parents I hid the evidence of my binges under my bed. I waited until I heard the familiar sound of my father snoring before I entered the kitchen and attacked the cupboards. It was easy to blame my sisters if too much food went astray. When I shared apartments with flatmates I would take care to replace their food should I devour it in a binge. If I was broke and could not afford to replace it I would point the finger at the absent third flatmate, complaining that half my food had gone missing too.

The humiliation of finding oneself surrounded by empty food wrappers whilst wearing a three-day-old T-shirt dripping with chocolate, gravy, lemon tart and half-cooked rice is a demeaning experience. Sitting by the fridge I was ashamed of my lack of control, disgusted by my excessive appetite and I felt the guilt working its way up my body. I could feel the fat attach itself to my body within minutes. My thighs were spreading and the sweat building beneath my bare breasts under the oversized T-shirt worn only for bingeing.

Big T-shirts, baggy sweaters, track-suit bottoms, baseball caps and dark glasses served as disguise when purchasing for a binge. The same disguise served as a binge uniform and nightwear when I went to bed. If a binge lasted three days then the outfit would remain the same. I could not have a shower for then I would be forced to view my body and my distorted body image ensured I would see truckloads of flesh falling from my arse, my thighs and my bloated tummy. I was disgusted with my lack of resolve and so I closed all the curtains, screened all calls and refused to answer the door.

In my bulimic days I would shove laxatives down my throat, swallowing packets at a time. In an attempt to rip my stomach out, strip my bowels bare and rid my body of the poison I had taken in I saw myself as meat, vast slabs of meat: flesh, fat and gristle.

I wanted to stop but I could not reveal my repulsive secret to anyone in case they walked away in disgust. So I continued shovelling food into my mouth by the saucepan-load, secretly wishing to be discovered but terrified that someone would see what I was doing. At these times the despair was overwhelming and the self-hatred overpowering. You could often find me sitting alone at two in the morning with crumbs floating in my tears, shocked at my own behaviour.

I set about developing advanced techniques in order to binge undetected. The risk of being caught out was always there but the desire to 'get away with it' was so great that the binge always won out and I was rarely, if at all, discovered.

A common question put to me is 'How did you get away with buying so much food; didn't anyone suspect anything?' As I have already said it takes a certain tenacity to be a binge eater.

A trolley filled with food in a supermarket is a standard sight but when you have a penchant for danish pastries and they simply must be from the only bakery of its kind in Sydney, then to purchase enough food for fifty on a daily basis can get a bit risky. To deflect the suspicion I would insist that I had come from the office block around the corner and had lost the list of goodies requested by my work colleagues. 'I can't remember what she wanted; you'd better make it two eclairs; he likes tarts so we'll get one of those, and a doughnut for the boss . . .' I'd inhale my imaginary office tea-break in my car in the back lane.

After four such visits I was concerned they would catch on so I wrote a dummy list and just handed it over the counter. It was years before it occurred to me that the bakery was in the middle of suburbia without an office block in sight. If I had realised it at the time I would have known I was caught out, as all dumb bulimics are sooner or later.

The truth is the checkout chick calculating the cost of your trolley-sized binge isn't thinking about how you are going to eat it all in one sitting; she's too busy worrying about her own life and whether her boyfriend is going to pick her up after work. Bulimia and binge eating are insular and private but the binge eater believes everyone can see through her; if she hates herself so much surely everyone else does too.

In desperation and a dire need to interrupt or stop the binge, I would find myself emptying the fridge of all temptation, throwing out fresh food so I would not weaken. Hours, sometimes days later as the desire to binge grew strong I would resort to scouring the bin for the food I had discarded.

There is a moment in every binger's life when things can't get any lower. Eating unthawed cake straight from the freezer was low but not low enough. For many it's the moment we find ourselves retrieving last night's doughnuts tossed in the bin in a fit of binge defiance, dusting off any cigarette ash, and eating the remains. I have heard of women who devoured tins of baby food meant for their newborn or their children's lunches left over in their school bags at the end of the day.

Throughout my twenty-odd years of bingeing I thought I would not get caught. So many people worked in the kitchens of Sydney and London that I believed they could never pin the disappearing desserts on me. The management of the advertising firm entrusted me with the petty cash and so long as it balanced each month they would never know how I spent the money.

At the old people's home they couldn't believe that anyone would sink so low as to steal the food from the inhabitants' trays. The Spastic Centre would never know that I was falsely collecting money unless someone told them, and all my friends cared about was getting food within the canteen-free school grounds. If I had been caught out in any of them I would have been mortified and immediately denied any participation even as the food stains dried on my face.

It was imperative that I denied all association with food and lived as if food was of no significance. When I ate with my friends I chewed on carrot sticks and said no to the slice of cake offered to me after school or in the office kitchen during coffee break. If they saw me eating they might connect the missing food with me and my fat body. I overcompensated for my bingeing, offering the girls in the playgrounds whatever treats my mother had packed and giving my workmates chocolates after lunch. I sacrificed my food for others in the hope they would make note that I did not eat and therefore could not be accused of stealing food I did not want.

What would I have done if I was discovered mid-binge? It never happened. But should my boyfriend/flatmate/boss/sister/mother have stumbled upon me surrounded by half-eaten trays of baklava, and melted Tim Tams with a Haagen Daaz masterpiece running down my shirt I would have died. That's what I believed. If my binge was revealed I simply would have ceased to exist. I could not imagine past the point of discovery. When I tried, everything went black.

Similarly if my true emotional turmoil had been revealed I would also have died, for it was the turmoil I was hiding with food, protecting myself from public humiliation by living in the third shelf of the fridge. I had no idea what came first, the despair or the binge, the binge or the despair; one fuelled the other. Before I went out at night I would hit my body with my fist, punishing my thighs for bulging from beneath my skirt, grabbing handfuls of stomach fat between my fingers and shaking hard: look, look at how base and gross you are! This punishment continued until the alcohol made me forget my extra rolls of fat.

The paranoia that accompanies food binges is something similar to drug-induced psychosis, because you suspect every person you meet knows that you have been eating. Often when I gave in to the cravings and the need to eat and eat and eat, I would leave the house unwashed, unshowered, wearing no underwear under baggy clothing, and as soon as I was out of the safety of my kitchen I would begin to feel self-conscious, convinced every person who passed me knew that I was bingeing.

When I purchased my next sweet or savoury fix I was

certain that the dealer behind the counter knew I was lying when I muttered something about 'family over for lunch' as I stumbled under the weight of twelve bagels, two shortbreads, a quiche and croissants. I would make a fast getaway to the safety of my car where I could not stuff the food in to my mouth fast enough, craving the brief but numbing high. A quick look in the rear-vision mirror just to make sure no one was following me, and I would be off in search of another fix.

These binges were followed by the need to salvage some respect, to rid myself of the effects of too much food – fat. A few hours of cramping torture and I would be purged. I combined my laxative abuse with exercise and took to the gym, running, cycling and boxing the binge off. I believed that exercise could bring me what dieting so far had not; the perfect body, and I took to it with gusto.

MIRROR MIRROR

WHERE'S MY GYM BRA and my leggings, for God's sake? My thighs are fucking enormous; look at them, they're stuck together.

I knew it; I've put on five kilos since yesterday. God, where are my car keys? If I just squat down and pull my T-shirt over my knees that should stretch it enough to cover my stomach and my arse.

I'll just have a cigarette on the way to silence those hunger pains. Wow, did you notice how your upper arms flap in the wind when you lean your arm out of the driver's window, Rach? That's disgusting. Better do some extra triceps today. Just look at them; if I hit my upper arm it won't stop wobbling till next week. Gross, I have cellulite on my arms.

Won't these lights ever change? For God's sake it's green missus, go, go, goooo! Bugger, you stupid cow, you could have gone then. Typical, she's a thin bitch behind the wheel of a Mercedes. Spent all her grocery money on the sunroof so she can get a tan while she drives. Skinny cow, bet she's had lipo.

I wonder if I lipo-ed my stomach where the fat would go to? If I had lipo from my entire body then surely the fat would have nowhere else to go and I could eat and eat and eat without ever putting on weight . . . or maybe my head would explode. Can you get fat nostrils? Or lips? Hey, if my lips got fat then I could save a fortune on collagen.

There's a spot!

That shopfront window can't be right: I look skinny. Nope, I knew it was a trick of the light, look at my shadow on the footpath. Any moron can see I need to lose ten kilos.

Oh look, that would-be-twelve-year-old with the peach skin and legs to the ceiling is on reception, and her five twin sisters are working with her.

'Good morning Rachael, haven't seen you for a while.'

Christ, what is her name? Una, Anja, Anna, Skinny Little White Chick with Big Tits? What does she mean she hasn't seen me for a while, does she have to point out to the whole world in reception that I am a lazy, fat cow who is losing muscle tone by the hour? Anyway you must be confusing me with some other heifer, I spent two and a half hours here yesterday. Oh God, maybe she doesn't recognise me because of the extra kilos.

'Here's the key to your locker and be sure to book in for our guest aerobics instructor next week. He's from Chicago and is a leader in the field of abs, hips and thighs.'

Thanks, Skinny Little White Chick. You can run home now, it's past your bedtime.

She's probably bonking the owner.

Man, it's crowded in here. Oh God, that woman has cellulite like mine and she's fifty! Oh Christ, she's got my upper arms!!! Must . . . get . . . air . . .

Must reach fat-burning level . . . Must reach fat-burning level . . . Must reach fat burning level . . . Wish I had a butt like the woman in front, it's tiny . . . Must reach fat-burning level . . . Must reach fat-burning level . . . Must reach fat-burning level.

How long have I been on this thing for now? Twelve minutes: burnt nine calories, rode half a kilometre . . . that can't be right, I haven't even burnt off the onion on last night's hot dog. Better put it up another level. Maybe my flatmate would go halves in the rent on a home gym. She'd probably get skinnier than me and then I would have to work out twice as hard so I looked better. Maybe I'll put the home gym in my bedroom so she can't use it.

Here they come, the aerobics brigade. What's that blonde wearing so much makeup for? It's not like the instructor is straight or anything.

They've opened the doors to the aerobics room. Better get inside and mark my spot with my towel. Oh God, I haven't done this class for ages; whose spot is where? Does that woman with the six-pack abs get the top front spot or does she take the side spot? Is my body good enough for the front row or should I go middle? I'm definitely not right in the back, that woman with the sagging stomach should go there. What if I've taken someone's spot already and I don't know it? I think I have, that woman is giving me the evil eye. Oh no she's not, she's looking past me at herself in the mirror.

If I stand too close to the front then the perfect bitches at the front will take notes on my arse but if I stand too far back then they'll think I'm not a regular. I don't know where to stand. Maybe I'll go out and come back in just as it starts and take whatever spot looks like it's not taken. Oh, then whoever usually has the spot I'm in will arrive late and seethe behind me for the rest of the class and I'll have to keep up with the instructor the whole way through just to justify my position at the front. Oh bollocks!

I could go to the back with the fat people and then I'd look skinny and I'm bound to be better at this than them so they can all think I'm fabulous even if I didn't colour co-ordinate my outfit today.

Oh look, the instructor's new. Haven't been to his class before, he'd better be good.

I love this song! I wish this woman in front would get out

of the way, who told her she could grapevine? Doesn't she know anything? That's an 'easy step', you fool! Watch out! You're bumping into me! Christ, if you can't co-ordinate yourself don't come to the class. Grapevine, darling, grapevine, that's better.

One, two, three, four, grapevine; one, two, three, four, easy step; one, two, three, four, grapevine.

I think I'll have a carrot juice for lunch.

One, two, three, four, walk to the front, clap; one, two, three, four, walk to the back, clap; one, two, three, four, clap – there's always one who gets it wrong, isn't there? Clap NOW – no, NOW!

Maybe I'll go on a ten-day juice fast. Then I can be really thin for Ashleigh's wedding and I can wear a slinky dress and be the belle of the ball. Her fiancé is bound to have some cute friends. Maybe I'll meet a stockbroker and marry him and live in New York. I could get married on Manhattan harbour, no, I'll do it here in Sydney first, then have a party in New York. What sort of cars should we get? White Jags could be nice. Depends on my dress really. Should I go for the straight, sleek and stylish or the princess? I'll have to go for the straight dress so I can dance, but if I still have these thighs then the princess dress would be better to hide the lumps. I couldn't get married if I was fat.

One, two, three, four . . .

William can do the flowers, he's such a great florist, and we can have a choir or an opera singer at the service. Black-and-white photos, they're far more flattering and easier to airbrush.

Oh dear, I can never do this 'mambo' thing properly. Hope my arse isn't wobbling.

I'll have to go out and buy a juicer, I'll stop at the fruit shop on the way home and stock up. If I'm going to meet a man and get married I had better look good.

'Great work ladies, now grab your weights and we'll do some upper-body work to keep those busts firm!'

Lift . . . lower . . . lift . . . lower

Carrot and celery juice would be the best; burns twice the calories when digesting.

How . . . many . . . more . . . of . . . these . . . triceps . . . do . . . we . . . have . . . to . . . do?

My stomach's sticking out a bit, maybe I'm pregnant. That could be it, that would explain the five kilos overnight, and my wobbly thighs, and my protruding belly. When's my period due?

Aagh . . . one . . . aagh . . . two . . . three . . . f . . . f . . . four . . .

I had it three weeks ago, or was it four? Where was I? That's right, Fiona's dinner party. When was that party? It must have been after the sales because I was wearing the size eight Scanlon skirt I bought for 50 per cent off; I haven't worn that since. I can't believe I bought it!

Hang on a second, I can't be pregnant, I haven't slept with anyone. That means I'm just fat. Fat and greedy, out of control. Maybe I'm pre-menstrual and bloated. Now when was my last period again?

Aagh . . . twenty . . . huahh . . . twenty one . . .

If I went on the pill then I would know when my next period is and I'll need to go on the pill if I'm getting married but then I'd put on weight and look pregnant so I might as well be pregnant anyway. Nah, smoking keeps my weight down and they say you can't smoke on the pill so I'd better forget that little idea, I might die from thrombosis of the knees. Thrombosis makes you really really fat and then I'd have to have a wide-berth coffin and I couldn't have a viewing because everyone would see how fat I was.

'Thanks, ladies, and don't forget to enrol for our guest aerobics instructor from Chicago . . .'

Yeah, yeah; you'd think the guest instructor was Anthony Robbins the way these women are signing up. Maybe I'd better not miss out, I mean he might turn out to be really good or something. But where will I stand in his class, and what if he thinks I'm un-co. Maybe I'll get his videotape out and practise at home first. Wonder how much the video is?

Typical, no showers vacant. That woman has definitely had a boob job, no doubt about it. Wonder how much they cost her? I wonder if it's more than a home gym or lipo?

These jeans feel a little bigger than last night. Hooray, I'm losing weight already. Imagine how big they'll be after my ten day fast. I don't look too bad actually. Stomach looks flatter than this morning.

'Bye, Rachael, have a good day.'

Thanks, Skinny Little Woman With Big Tits, I think I shall. Now where's the fruit market? Down the escalator and turn left.

Oh God, I don't really look like that, do I? Who was I kidding? Look at my thighs in that shopfront window, they're worse than this morning. What was I thinking? I can't go out like this.

Gym junkie, that was me. My life revolved around 6 a.m. boxing, 5 p.m. pump, 6.30 p.m. step and 8 p.m. circuit. I admired my muscle tone daily as I lifted my leg above my head in the morning, flexing my quads. 'You know I can't come for drinks at 6, I have got a 5.30 p.m. abs, hips and thighs class. I don't care if it's the last time I'll see you before you move interstate; I just can't miss that class, OK?' I loathed my body and filled my home with mirrors, bathroom scales and photos of genetic freaks-on-catwalks just so I could loathe it some more.

With two personal trainers, a private tennis coach, a nutritionist, naturopath, acupuncturist and allergy consultant (I am not exaggerating) I still looked in the mirror and saw Lard Arse. I wanted the Perfect Body and was happy to sacrifice my time, my social life, my work, my friends, my health to get it.

The Perfect Body does exist, you know – I have photos on my fridge to prove it. It has been sighted on the catwalks of

Milan, in the pages of Sports Illustrated and on lingerie commercials adorning the sides of buses. The Perfect Body (PB) is a symmetrical vision of long legs, concave stomach, C cup breasts, tiny buttocks, collarbones, ribs and hipbones and is usually topped with white teeth, upturned nose, big lips and large open eyes above cliff-like cheekbones. The PB is always underweight and overtall.

Everybody knows that the PB is better than the AB (Average Body) which is always overweight and undertall. The further from the Average Body and the closer to the Perfect Body you are then the better you are. You can gauge how far away you are from the PB by looking at other women and comparing your body to theirs and theirs to the PB.

The Perfect Body is totally achievable. Every woman can create it. It takes self-discipline to achieve the perfect body. 'No pain, no gain.' You have to 'make it burn'. The gym, the plastic surgeon and diet gurus can help you achieve the Perfect Body.

The Perfect Body brings with it the Perfect Life. With the Perfect Body you will be loved by men with killer cheekbones, your long legs will brush the seats of European cars, you will want for nothing and be surrounded by other BLPs (Beautiful Laughing People).

When working towards the Perfect Body, remember the mirror always lies. Don't trust it. Whatever it tells you, it will be wrong. If it says you are thin, it's lying. The only mirrors that tell the truth are in communal change rooms under fluorescent lights. They are the only mirrors that do not lie.

Do not believe a word a skinny woman says to you; the skinnier the woman the bigger the bitch. She thinks she's fat and you know you are. Tell her she's put on weight and she'll run screaming in the opposite direction and leave you in peace.

Remember it is possible to put on seven kilos in twenty-four hours and that loss of control means loss of body. Your body must be patrolled all day every day in shopfront windows, rear vision mirrors, and other people's sunglasses lest it try to break free.

It is better to die than be fat; any woman should know that. Cigarettes will disguise all hunger pains and when choosing an entrée go for the oysters as they may give you food poisoning and help you lose your burgeoning thighs.

Elle Macpherson has the Perfect Body and it is possible to look like her regardless of genetics. Plaster her on your fridge door, bathroom mirror, the back of the bedroom door, behind the sun visors of your car.

When it comes to the quest for the Perfect Body men are not to be trusted. A man will never tell you when you have put on weight, he will say you look 'fine' when you know you are losing the battle and he will say you look 'tired' when you are winning. When he does say he thinks you look terrific, beautiful, stunning and thin then he only wants to get you into bed. Women are also not to be trusted as they will always lie about your body, particularly skinny women.

If you don't have the Perfect Body then you will have Bad Body Image (BBI) because you don't have the Perfect Body. But don't fret; everybody has BBI. How many times have you heard your best friend lament 'I'm so fat; I have put on five kilos since yesterday' as she stands in front of you as skinny as a child? When the going gets tough the Bad Body Imagers go to the mirror to find the source of the pain. 'My boyfriend dumped me – I'm so fat. My boss is a bitch – I'm so fat. My mother is nagging me – I'm so fat. My best friend's getting married – I'm so fat. I'm so fat, I'm so fat, I'm so fat.' We all know it is because they don't have the PB that their life is a mess and without the PB then we are left with BBI.

Should you find yourself with BBI then you will already have invested in the truth that perfection exists in the physical form (the PB), that perfection is better and that you can get that perfection by changing your physical self. Changing your physical self can be done through dieting, shopping, and plastic surgery.

Body-issue babes are prone to excess. For a bulimic or binge eater the binge is excessive; the anorexic starves herself to excess. Purging presents its own level of excess in direct ratio to the size of the binge. The bigger the binge, the bigger the purge.

I have always been an excessive individual: excessively hungry, an excessive spender and excessive drinker. My motto for most of my life was 'if you're going to do it, do it with excess'. I knew no other way to live. From a young age I was given all I wanted and when I wasn't given it I would take it anyway, believing it was mine for the grabbing and my parents had no right to say no.

Some would say I was one of those annoying people who knew everything. Of course I disagree. It's just that if someone had a story I had one better. I was an expert on sky diving, even though I had done it just once. Of course my brief sojourn in advertising made me an expert on marketing and my two-week course in photography made me Annie Liebowitz. If I had met myself at a party I would have run in the opposite direction. Instead I threw the parties, ensuring they were the most outrageous and most talked about for years.

When you have The Gaze, then Bad Body Image and the Perfect Body don't exist. The Gaze is all about being looked at by others and looking at others. Bad Body Image comes about by comparing yourself to the Perfect Body and determining how close you are or are not to the PB by looking at other bodies around you. You will always have The Gaze as others look at you to see where you fit in relation to the PB. Do you have it? Do they have it? Who wants it and who has got it? Some have more of The Gaze than others and some have less. If you have BBI then you will always have The Gaze from yourself as you look at others and then look back at yourself again. Still with me? Good.

The anorexic has perfected The Gaze and forces others to look at the suffering on her body. Look at me and see how much pain I am in. The more she loses the more attention she creates.

The compulsive overeater wants to hide in her body, does not want anyone to look, does not look herself and, like the anorexic, displays her own pain and suffering on her frame. The bigger she becomes the more comments she creates. She has The Gaze and hates herself for it. Negative comments from strangers, friends and family only fuel the negative thoughts about herself.

Without constant comparison between our bodies and the bodies on the billboards and television, then BBI would not exist. Continuous comparison between the body we have now and the body we had yesterday, or last week, or last year. Look at her body, look at ours, see how ours pales in comparison.

I have spent entire weekends inside my home, too ashamed to go out, because my mirror told me I was fat. When I did go out, I felt my stomach triple in size between 7 p.m. and 10 p.m. before I ran home in disgust, catching sight of my waves of flesh in the shop windows. I would start dieting two weeks before a hair appointment because I could not bear to sit in front of my image for three hours straight. If I did not get a wink from the bridge toll collector on my way into town for a night out, I would turn around and go home to redo my hair. Mirrors, shop fronts, toll collectors and drunken men in bars all became the indicators I measured my body and closeness to perfection by. When I was not perfect I could always beat my body harder with four-hour aerobic sessions, cellulite pummelling and steam torture.

I am a sucker for The Gaze. I have to be the most

beautiful at a party. If I am not, then I must be the loudest, the funniest, the best dressed. I am willing to pay a far higher price than most for that limited commodity. At school I did lunchtime break-dancing for The Gaze, I locked myself in cupboards during English class and I dieted. When school was over I worked in radio and television, seeking The Gaze of thousands. Look at me, look at me, look at me. If someone else had The Gaze I would get louder, funnier, thinner to take The Gaze which I believed was mine.

This desire for The Gaze made me an ideal candidate for a job in the media. When I returned home after three-and-a-half years in London I talked my way into a job as a radio announcer and then as a television presenter to ensure I got The Gaze. I lapped up the attention from listeners, from record company reps who wanted me to play their music, from bands I interviewed. I got free clothes, free CDs, free movie tickets and invitations to parties.

But The Gaze does have a price. Too much Gaze can cause discomfort. No one can have The Gaze 100 per cent of the time. The Gaze is addictive: the more you have the more you want, and, like an addict, you may resort to stealing The Gaze from others for your fix.

My desire for the Perfect Body and in turn The Gaze created a backlash of Bad Body Image when I posed naked for a national women's magazine. How I got talked into stripping for a woman's magazine I do not know. Well, I do actually, all it took was for them to ask. A journalist friend was writing an article on people and their bedrooms: shots of women in satin surrounded by teddy bears from their childhood days, men in leather sleeping next to their stereos, quotes from the bedroom owners on how they spent their time in the bedroom, what their bedroom meant to them, that sort of thing. Rach was to be the ethereal woman with the mystical bedroom all in flowing white. That's what I had in my mind anyway.

My friend interviewed me, encouraging me to tell her the wildest stories from my bedroom. I did not need much encouragement. After all I must be the wildest one interviewed if I wanted The Gaze to be on me instead of the others in the story. I regaled her with stories of séances, seduction and sex on the windowsill, forever embellishing the story to fantasy-like proportions. Then came the photo shoot.

By the time the black-clad art director arrived on my doorstep I had adorned myself in funky attire ready to dazzle the camera lens. Needn't have bothered really. A quick suggestion from the art director that I pose naked was enough. I didn't want to lose face in front of these style-meisters.

I wanted to appear hip and unfazed, as if I took my clothes off for complete strangers with attitude all the time (I know, I know). I reclined my naked body across my king-sized bed. I was imagining how my daring nude photo shoot would become a cocktail hour anecdote when the photographer asked me to flip over onto my other side.

You try positioning yourself while stark naked – it ain't easy. If I moved to the left then my breasts would have sagged to the right; if I looked downward seductively at the camera then my chins would have multiplied. Honestly, I had so many individual concerns running through my brain it took until the style police had packed up and gone before I realised I'd been had. Good old Rach, they must have laughed themselves stupid on the way back to the studio. 'All we had to do was suggest that it was better for the story if she showed some flesh and before you could say "sucker" she'd stripped off.'

I calmed my nerves with a loaf of banana bread and a Wendy's soft-serve icecream. I acted cool and nonchalant, boasting to my friends about my daring eccentricity and complete comfort with my body. Secretly I had plans to buy up all the issues and donate them to the Australian School for the Blind.

The issue hit the streets, complete with mammoth title page shot of little old innocent Rach displaying her wares for all to see. I was filled with ambivalent emotions. Elated that I was the star of the story and I had The Gaze, guilty that I had exposed so much of myself to get it.

When I shot the story for this leading women's mag I wanted everyone to look at me but deciding to go naked had its repercussions. Choosing to go to such extremes to ensure all eyes were on me led to a three-month backlash binge and an extra seven kilos in weight.

I was choosing to compete for The Gaze when I lay on my bed naked that day. This photo shoot and all the attention it would bring would make me better than my girlfriends, would have the girls at the radio station envious, and my sisters seething. I didn't strip off so men could see me. I stripped off so women in my life could envy me my daring position in the limelight and my smooth bottom.

TILL DIET DO US PART

SO LET ME GET THIS STRAIGHT. God created Adam, Adam's ribs created Eve, Eve got hungry and dared to eat from the Tree of Knowledge (Geez . . . if He didn't want Eve to eat from the Tree of Knowledge of Good and Evil then why didn't He call it the Insignificant Shrub of No Importance?). And as a result, I am now being condemned for Eve's hunger and am destined to excruciatingly and long hours of childbirth for all eternity. Now that makes sense.

Just like Eve, it is my appetite for the forbidden that has caused my downfall. If I had not eaten all those sumptuous fruits, not participated in those postcoital Hagen Daaz binges, not eaten breakfast, lunch AND dinner, I would never have gotten fat and 'he' wouldn't have left me. If I had just ignored that hankering for breakfast this morning I would not have put on five kilos and it would be me beaming for the camera, instead of that blonde pre-pubescent excuse for a would-be famine victim.

Every woman knows that hunger is a sin. Thank God I'm not Catholic or I would have spent my entire waking life between the four walls of a confessional instead of the four walls of the Westinghouse Frost Free.

Sometimes, when I am at a gathering of women, I feel as

though I am surrounded by Eves as we all dutifully ignore the tempting plates of pastries oozing with custard, the array of bagels spilling avocado, mayonnaise and chicken, the antipasto dripping in oil. When asked to bring a plate, like serpents we pile our plates high to tempt the other women to reveal their forbidden appetite. None of us game enough to eat and all of us returning home to stick our heads in the fridge and eat ourselves stupid. Yet in public when offered bites from the plate of temptation we deliver our well-rehearsed lines . . .

'No thank you, I ate yesterday.'

Subtext: Actually I ate all through yesterday because I was so anxious about what you people would think of me today. I hope you've noticed my BMW keyring on the table. Where's the toilet? I need to throw up.

'I'll only have the one bite, would you like to split a slice?'

Subtext: I don't want you putting two and two together and thinking I am fat because I eat. I can't wait to get home and get out of this skirt. I should never have worn Lycra.

'Danish? No, I couldn't possibly, I have been ever so bad lately, I feel huge.'

Subtext: I had that Tim Tam yesterday and I just know that's why my thighs feel fat. I wonder how long this lunch goes on for. I have a personal training session at two. I suppose I could have a slice of danish if I run an extra two kilometres today and skip dinner but I'll eat it in the toilet, I don't want anyone watching.

'Really, you must all eat. Please try some of the antipasto, it's delicious.'

Subtext: God, I hope they don't leave all this food. I can't trust myself around it, I'll have to throw it in the bin. Garbage night isn't till Wednesday and I just can't control myself with a bin full of danishes. I'll have to feed them to the dog.

Like good little Eves we don't eat in public, keeping our hunger hidden and preferring the privacy of our own kitchen of Eden in which to devour the forbidden apple. We share the same physiology, the XX chromosomes and the joys of childbirth but we can't share a danish at a party of women without judgement.

As women, our bodies are our measuring tools. They measure how much better or worse we are by comparison to other women, they control how we feel in a gathering of other girls: superior or inferior. How many times have you met a boyfriend's ex-girlfriend and exhaled with relief when you realised you are thinner or more beautiful? We put other women down by comparison ('Ooh look, her ankles are fat') to make ourselves feel better about our own bodies, then we feel guilty about putting them down and compare ourselves again to make ourselves feel better, or we eat to swallow the guilt.

How many hours have you spent shopping for a frock for a black-tie function so you can be the most glamorous, the prettiest or the best dressed? But ask a man what you or any of the other women were wearing and he probably could not tell you. Ask a woman who was at the same function and she'll tell you the cut and the cost and throw in the calorie allowance for every woman there.

Other women are imperative to dieting, and not just for comparison either. Where would a girl be without a Diet Pal to hold hands with on the tortuous road to thin thighs, concave stomachs and sunken cheeks? Every woman knows dieting life is exhausting. If we're not counting the calories, we're counting the fat; if it's not the fat then we're weighing the food; when we're not weighing food we're weighing ourselves. There's the vitamin supplements to measure, the zone to stay in, twenty minutes of cardio followed by fifteen of fat-burner. A girl needs a full-time food accountant just to keep up. That's where the Diet Pal comes in handy. Control is everything and you don't want to miscalculate a single kilojoule; it could mean the difference between a size eight and a size eight and a bit. Handing over the control to a Diet

Pal ensures no nasty slip-ups. A shared diet tip or a mutual lament over weight not lost can join women together for life.

'Do you, Rachael Oakes-Ash, take Andrea Beckett as your lawfully wedded Diet Pal? To calorie count, weigh and measure from this day forward?'

'I do.'

'Do you promise to admonish her, to hit her with a wet teatowel or a bag of frozen peas when a forbidden morsel passes her lips, to drag her kicking and screaming on a 5 a.m. run, to take away her own free food will and remind her of the empowering qualities of psyllium husk, beetroot juice and radish dip on a daily basis?'

'I do.'

'Do you, Andrea Beckett, take Rachael Oakes-Ash as your Diet Master? To fear and betray, to sacrifice taste, pleasure and nutrition to from this day forward?'

'I do.'

'Do you promise to eat rice three times a day, drink an elephant's share of water and answer Rachael's 3 a.m. phone calorie questions until diet do you part?'

'I do.'

'I now pronounce you Diet Pals. You may deprive your tastebuds for life.'

As Diet Pals, Andrea and I went on Fit for Life, the Atkins Weight-Loss Program and the Liver Cleansing Diet – an eight-week denial program with foul-smelling green tonic to be administered each morning. Phone calls were made to each other every half hour, checking in on current calorie intake. 'Do you think my liver's looking good by now?'

'Bugger the liver, I've lost an inch round my waist from the bowel-cleaning effects of the tonic alone!' Our social lives were reduced to videos and a microwaved potato on Saturday night.

One Friday night, in the fifth week of liver cleansing, I dropped in to say goodbye to an Irish girlfriend of mine before she returned to her homeland. Petrified of my own appetite and lack of control I arrived two hours early so I wouldn't be there to witness dinner. As Sara diced and chopped, concocting carpaccios, melting mushrooms and creaming canapés I stood wedged in the corner of the kitchen snacking on snap-sealed packets of freshly cut carrots, celery and radish from within my handbag. Sara knew how to create gourmet meals with the twitch of her nose. She offered me a drink as she cooked.

'A vodka and lime? I'm not sure. May I use your phone?

'Hi Andrea? It's me, Rach. Did you have anything to drink last night when you went out? . . . You did . . . Great, so what did you have? . . . Was that slimline tonic or regular? . . . Just the one or did you have more? . . . No, no, you can tell me; I promise I won't be mad . . . All right, all right . . . So, it would be fair to say you had three . . . and a cocktail – was that creamy or sour? . . . Reduced fat or full cream? . . . Were those strawberries canned in sugar syrup or fresh? . . . So, three vodkas and tonic and one full-cream cocktail but with fresh strawberries . . . Okay, great, thanks, Andrea . . . Yep, I'll see you at 6.15 tomorrow morning for Body Burn and then a twelve-mile power walk . . . No, Andrea, you have to be there . . . So what if it's Sunday? You're not religious . . . Ciao, ciao!

Sara, I will have that vodka and lime, thanks.

I beg your pardon? Do I want cheese and crackers with that?

Uh, hang on a tick while I just use your phone . . .'

Food held my friendships together. I knew I could rely on one friend to diet with and another to binge. I knew which women would join me in my quest for peak physical fitness and who would partner me in the post-marathon food binge. I knew my Diet Pals from my Binge Pals and who to call in moments of crisis.

I saw my Binge Pals on weekends when I was willing to let go, spending Saturday night bingeing on booze and

Sunday on chocolate, ice cream and all other foods forbidden during the week.

My girlfriends and I spent years competing for the ultimate body. We ate carrots in the schoolyard and crammed doughnuts in our homes as we raced towards the finish line, unaware of what we were really competing for. We welcomed other women who wrestled with their bodies and exiled those who did not.

'I really mustn't have one of those slices. I have put on seven kilos and am terribly disappointed with myself.'

'Ooooh, you too? I've been having awful trouble trying to shift the weight from my last baby.'

'Have you tried the new diet? It's the You Too Can Look like Gwyneth Paltrow Diet.'

'No, I've been dying to try it, a cousin of mine did it and you wouldn't recognise her now.'

Voilà, instant friends! But for how long?

If I always had someone else to diet with, to run with, to pound my body and my mouth with, then I thought I wouldn't feel so alone in my quest. God forbid that my Diet Pal should weigh less than me, lose more weight than me, be more dedicated to the diet cause than me. If she was winning the Diet Game and getting ahead of me then I would resort to sabotage: food pushing, encouraging my Diet Pal to partake of a slice of chocolate cake or five in the hope the weight would creep back on and I could once again be leader of the Diet Game.

Girls, beware the Food Pusher. Usually obsessed with her own body, the Food Pusher will become obsessed by yours, particularly if you are thin, beautiful and have a man. These women understand temptation; they fight against it every day. In order to achieve their envied thin position they hit the competition where it hurts: their bodies. These women think nothing of stomping their stilettos over any girl in the way.

They know the knee-weakening qualities of a chocolate

mud cake with King Island cream, they are familiar with the power of a succulent lemon tart encased with melt-in-your-mouth shortbread pastry and they are not afraid to use them. Immaculately dressed, with a waspish waist and firm breasts, the Food Pusher will constantly complain of imaginary fat ('I am so huuuuge'). She will even pretend to eat the temptations she has whipped up for your 'enjoyment'.

Even as you inhale the mud cake dripping in chocolate fudge the Food Pusher is already cutting you a second slice and moving her own untouched piece around on the plate. Occasionally she might raise her silver fork to her pencilled lips but usually she'll run to the bathroom straight after such an occasion. The Food Pusher denies her own yearnings and plays on yours. She knows her hunger is her downfall and she makes a pretty safe bet that your hunger will be yours.

It's been going on for centuries, this competition dressed up as friendship, but the twenty-first century chick has established a new battleground in which to play. The Diet Game. It keeps us from relating to each other, from relating to ourselves and from taking our power back. It's alive in the home, it's alive in the playground and it's alive in the workplace.

The rules of the Diet Game are simple. You must be a woman to play and the aim is to lose the most weight. You lose a turn when you put on weight, but you can always get back into the game the next time round.

My girlfriends and I went round after round of the Diet Game, picking up half a diet here, three aerobic classes there. When we were really driven just before summer we'd play our 'get out of fat farm free' cards. The aim was to own all the diet secrets and finish the race the thinnest.

'And they're off and running, Thunder Thighs Thelma is first off the mark, Trying Not To Eat Tina is not far behind, A Lettuce A Day Leanne is coming up the rear as they hit the hundred metre mark. Number Twelve, I'm Starving Susan, stops for a food break . . . Thin As A Bean Belinda has fallen behind; Thunder Thighs Thelma still leads by an inch, A Lettuce A Day Leanne has fallen away, clearing the track for Give Me That Gateau Gail as she makes a break for the lead. Trying Not To Eat Tina has lost her footing . . . Give Me That Gateau Gail is fighting it out with Thunder Thighs Thelma as they enter the straight – it's Thunder Thighs Thelma, Give Me That Gateau Gail, Calorie Counting Carol. Ooh; it's a photo finish with Calorie Counting Carol leading by a kilojoule.'

Have you noticed how a pack of women react when one of their own loses more than a kilogram? Pouncing on her in their eagerness to do the same. 'How much did you lose? What did you eat? What is your secret? How did you get away with it? Was that one enema or two?' Out come the notebooks in the belief that this time they really can drop two sizes in a week.

Try listening in to those same women an hour later, now sipping on their skinny decaf cappuccinos and devouring triple-chocolate mud cake. 'She'll never keep it off'. 'I heard she was bulimic'. 'No, it's because Jonathon dumped her'. 'She's on cocaine, you can see it in her eyes'. 'Her ribs were sticking out, that's so gross'. 'I heard she is a lesbian, is there any more cake?'

During my time as Chief of Diet Police I took time out to relax at a beach resort. My Diet Pal, Andrea, had arranged a spacious apartment with all the mod cons and a view of the ocean. Andrea unpacked her stilettos, her sequins and her silk as I unloaded my bag of my Nikes, bike shorts and heart monitor. We obviously had different holidays in mind.

Andrea spent the first day sussing out the nightclubs, bars and restaurants as I made friends with the owner of the health store, checked out the gym equipment and did a five kilometre run. I fed us organic porridge in the morning. I refused all alcohol and insisted Andrea refuse it with me. I was devastated when I awoke to find Andrea and a strange man in a Sambuca haze on the sofa bed.

She had let me down. She had dared to go out, break the rules, have a good time, drink alcohol, eat chips and get laid. How could she do this to me? Now I was alone. Just me, my 100 per cent natural oats and my size eight hipster pants. As the Chief of Diet Police I had failed to place her under house arrest. My diet fugitive had gone AWOL, she was missing in action and having a ball. I envied Andrea her stilettos and vodka and limes because she was doing what I was terrified of. She had let go.

It wasn't just dieting that linked me with my female friends and kept me part of the pack. Bingeing, drug taking, clothes shopping and men all kept us glued together as friends. We'd meet for drinks, or drugs, or food or retail therapy then discard our five years of friendship as we fought over men.

My single girlfriends and I devoured the town every Saturday night. We entered the bar comrades, betrayed each other in battle and linked up again when we left empty handed. Sundays were then spent debriefing over tubs of ice cream and pizza: curtains closed, TV on, door shut tight.

Keeping face in the Diet Game means putting the pressure on each other to remain slim and beautiful. We never admit when it is just too goddamn tough to work five days a week, change twenty-five nappies and keep the mould from the bathroom lest another player pounce on our weakness. It's hard enough keeping a smile on the face at the end of a ten hour shift, let alone unsmudged foundation, powder, mascara and lipstick. It's difficult enough staring cross-eyed at a computer screen for eight hours straight without having to stare at our bulging bum in the mirror. But you would never know any of this from your fellow competitors.

Dieting has nothing to do with men. Dieting is all about other women. I'm a feminist who hates women, at least today. Hell, at times I loathe women. Double hell, many times I can't stand to be near them. The problem is, I have spent so much time competing with them that I just don't know how to relate to them anymore. It's not the women that repulse me; it's my reaction to them. I don't feel like a feminist when I eye up the new woman being introduced at Friday night drinks. I survey her body, searching for a bump, a lump, an overhang of flesh, a fault, something I can jump on to make myself feel better about who I am and my position in the group. Nor do I feel like a feminist when I secretly gloat at another woman's weight gain after a death in her family. I certainly don't feel like a feminist when I flaunt my freshly slimmed-down body in the hospital as I congratulate my friends on the birth of their babies.

I hate women who move in on my man, I despise women who would scramble over their grandmother to get to the cute guy in the corner. I call myself a woman's woman, rant and rave about equal rights, yet I seethe if I am not the best-dressed at the party.

Thirteen-year-old girls with their peachy skin, flirty skirts and innocent eyes make me sick.

I loathe anorexics. I want to shake them and tell them to put on weight. I want to point out that the baggy clothes hide nothing (and I should know). I want to scream at those anorexics wearing Lycra to stop rubbing their body in my face, to grow up, to take hold of themselves. I want to tell them they're martyrs – pathetic and they make me sick. I feel enormous next to anorexics; I feel they are judging my fat as lazy, slovenly, out of control. They remind me of myself and I can't bear to stare directly at their self-destruction.

In the past I have been known to whoop with glee at my friends' traumas, when they don't get the job, the house or the car. Thank God, I sigh with relief, they are not getting ahead of me, I still have time. Then I am racked with so much guilt I offer them my job, my house or my car. I have no idea how to stand my ground and gracefully take what is mine, and how to share the rest. I scream about equal pay and scream louder when I find my girlfriends are earning more than me.

It's not the men that worry me when the top of my hipster skirt is sitting up around my waist. It's the chicks, my girlfriends, the women, the gals – what will they say? I know they'll say something, they will check me out, calculate how much I have put on and smile sweetly as they tell me how fabulous I look. I will know they are lying when I feel their eyes in the back of my buttocks as I waddle over to the bar for a drink.

I used to have the chauvinist qualities of men on a building site, eyeing women as they walked in front of me. But I was looking for visible panty line, a wobbly piece of flesh or rolls of fat over the back of the bra. Sussing out the competition, seeing what does and doesn't work and betraying womankind with my judgments.

In a family of four women I learnt early on how to keep other women happy. The days spent shopping for the flashiest dress, must-have mules, latest make-up and hip-hugging pants were about dressing for women, not men. The weight loss, the diets, the gym workouts are about being smaller, more glamorous, better-looking than the girl on the Stairmaster next to you. Tell any girl they've lost weight and they are your friend for life; imply they may have put on a stray kilo or two and watch the nails come out.

As for friends, I always chose women who were too much. They would control too much, or give too much, or need too much, or drink too much, eat too much, starve too much, screw around too much . . . I never made the connection to my own reflection. By competing with these women for the ultimate body, the ultimate man, the ultimate job, ultimate invite, ultimate home I was preventing myself from living the ultimate life.

When my girlfriends chose to go on a date instead of hang out with me I would seethe with my rejection. I expected them, like my mother, to be there at my beck and call, to soothe my pain, to counsel my grief, to service me endlessly. When they dared to have a life of their own I would stamp my foot and give them the cold shoulder, punishing them for their betrayal. 'It's outrageous the way she drops everything for a man. She has no life. I haven't heard from her since they started going out. I'm sure she'll call when he dumps her. She's so needy. She's lost weight. Can't be eating. Won't last long.' I could have been describing myself.

Of course it is one thing to gloat over our friends' misfortunes and another to witness the downfall of the truly beautiful girl and her PB. There falls the image we cling to as we flick through the glossy tabloids at the supermarket checkout. Those skinny girls in sequins with their perfect lives are our inspiration as we unload our trolley of no-taste-no-fat milk, diet soda, celery sticks and double-coated-choc-dipped Tim Tams. Imagine our horror and empathy when these beautiful women reveal cracks in their 'gl-armour'.

Oh hell, who am I kidding? I loved it when Kate lost her gloss, I relished the dimples in Demi Moore's thighs, I have an orgasm every time Gwyneth is dumped. I dream about Courtney Cox going into therapy for compulsive overeating and I would kill to see any number of bottle-blonde television stars fall flat on their aerobicised arses.

Why? Because I've always been matt, not gloss. My thighs resemble a crate of oranges, I've been dumped more times than Gwyneth has had hot dinners, and I could have bought a brand new small car with the money I've spent on therapy.

I loathe women on television that I have never met, simply because they have lost weight. I abhor women I do not know simply because they have had the self-control to stop eating (never mind the fifty-thousand-dollar-a-year personal trainer and live-in low fat chef). Why can't I do that? I look to the handful of overweight celebrities to tell me I am okay, that there is hope, that I can look glamorous, that I can have a career, a lover, a laugh and when they lose weight I am let down. Shame on you, Sophie Dahl. How could you, Roseanne?

I would pay money to see Melanie Griffiths' lips explode, Madonna's butt hang low, Jennifer Aniston's hair fall out. There is no sisterhood when it comes to celebrities. I feel absolutely no obligation to stand by their side, to march in the streets and hold sit-ins in Hollywood when they are not there supporting my own struggle in the kitchen. The thinner they get, the more they ignore their hunger, the more betrayed I feel.

It is hard to act like glamorous Barbie in this world when you feel like Raggedy Anne, to remain on tiptoes, always smiling, always pert. Permanently standing on tiptoes hurts.

When I was seventeen and anorexic I felt like a doll. Stiff, painted, hollow. I had believed the hype that Barbie and her cohorts offered me as a child; I believed the promise of love, happiness and fortune that the weight loss infomercials guaranteed night after night and I was bitterly disappointed when it didn't happen. I felt cheated and had no idea how to show my hunger. I was thin, plastic and glamorous and I was not eating. I fed on my insides until I became a walking cavity, a plastic caricature of the cover girl glamour puss I strived to be.

I am beginning to sound like Adam, blaming Eve for all my troubles instead of taking responsibility for my own insatiable hunger for life, for love, for attention. But hey, I am hungry and I do want it all, I want the fairytale princess life; what girl doesn't? I want to devour all the glamorous jobs, I want to inhale all the fabulous designer rags, suck on all the parties, and I want all the eyes of millions of souls worldwide pointed at me so I can bask in the radiance of their adoring gaze and, just quietly, I don't want anyone else to have it either.

I spent years trying to emulate Barbie, promising myself that this time, this day I would be positive, happy and glowing. Needless to say by mid-morning I'd be hauling up my drooping tights, cursing the man who invented the stiletto and wiping my Chanel Vamp smile off my front teeth for the fifth time that day. As I kicked the vending machine for a Diet Coke I would be dreaming of Mars Bars. I wandered the corridors of wherever I was working at the time smiling sweetly, carrying my black I-look-intelligent Filofax, pulling in my non-existent tummy and secretly doing pelvic-floor crunches in the team meeting. But it wasn't working; something had to give (besides my elasticised firm-top panties). I couldn't go on starving myself forever.

I had no idea how to express my hunger in a moderate manner, how to reach for what satisfied me and leave it at that. I always had to go one step further. My hunger was constantly being suppressed so when I did reach out I tried to grab the biggest piece I could imagine.

When I finally did learn to express my hunger at the time I felt it and not leave it bottled up and neglected, I found that I didn't want as much as I had been trying to take. But re-creating my own world took longer than God's seven days.

GO FIGURE

Life? Oh, it's great, you know. Couldn't be better. Yes, yes, it's me you heard on the radio. Oh, you saw me on telly too? And in the paper? That would have been the social pages, out with my new man. Yes, he is famous. Thank you, yes, I have been this size for a number of years now. It's my personal trainers, they do an amazing job. This year's season, darling, it's fab, isn't it? I thought the camera did it justice. The tan? Just back from Thailand. The magazine? Oh, that little piece, tongue-in-cheek of course. The bedroom is fabulous. Yes, it's waterfront – should say harbourfront really; magnificent view in the morning. Life? Couldn't be better. Must go; have a photo shoot at ten, lunch with agent at one, on location at three and in the studio at six. Ciao, ciao!

Life? Oh, it's great, you know. Couldn't be better. No, no, not on the radio any more. Yes, yes, bit of a scandal but these things happen. Yes, yes, still doing TV. No, no, just go to the gym now. Personal trainers were getting a bit Nazi on me, you know how it is. This little number? Last season, but don't tell anyone. The tan? Solarium, darling, does wonders for the complexion. Yes, yes, still with the man. You saw him? Where? With who? No, no, must have been his sister. Oh, blonde, you say? No, I got sick of the harbour view, one tends to get so complacent, doesn't one? Upgraded to a two bedroom apartment, sick of all that lawn to mow. Life? Couldn't be better. Must go, interviewing prospective agents at three. Ciao, ciao!

Life? Oh, it's great, you know. Couldn't be better, no, really, it couldn't. No, no, haven't actually heard the girl on the radio who took my place. I hear she's not that great, bit young. TV? Left that, didn't want to be overexposed, can't be too careful. This old thing? Just a grunge promo T-shirt, I was ducking out the shops for milk, you know how it is, didn't expect to see anyone. Yes, a couple of kilos, I'm sure they'll shift in summer when I get a tan. The man? No, no, we broke up. He didn't want commitment . . . but then of course neither did I, so it all worked out. No, no, I'm not upset at all. Job? Oh, I'm temping, just needed some time out, schedule was too hectic. Life? Couldn't be better. Must go, interviewing for a new flatmate at four. Ciao, ciao!

Life? Oh, it's fucking great, you know. I stink. Haven't showered for four days. Can't get out of bed. Try to move my arm, nothing happens. So angry. Hungry, can't move. Food. What's in the fridge? Cheese, ice cream, chocolate biscuits. Ate them all last night. Can't get out of bed. Need to get to the shops. Fuck it. My thighs, my stomach, my arse, spreading over the bedsheets. Empty wrappers by my bed, crumbs rubbed into my pillow. This is so fucking gross. I'm pathetic. Can't get out of bed. Grime on my skin, carpet mouth, hair matted and greasy. Dandruff, blackheads, plaque. What time is it? Can't get out of bed. I'm so pitiful, pathetic. Fat, fucking fat. Washing sitting in the machine wet since last week's cycle, can't move, can't get out of bed. Can hear my flatmate in the shower, singing, happy fucking bitch. Hurry up and leave. I have to be alone in my pity. Legs unshaven, underarms stink, itchy pubes, grotty toes, half-wiped bum. Sleep, must sleep some more. Phone, it's ringing, probably work. Fuck off, I'm not coming in. Last night's pizza, it's in the bin. It's still in the box, should be able to wipe it off and heat it up. Door slam. Flatmate's gone. Can't get out of bed. Tears, sobs, pain, I'm so pathetic. Help me, someone help me. Life? Couldn't be fucking better. Must go, have an appointment with the fridge in five minutes. Ciao fucking ciao!

Me? I'm famous you know. Well, it's been a while. I'm sure you remember me. I was the chick on the radio each night. No, I didn't do the weather. Oh, you must have been away that year. I've met Janet Jackson. No, not her brother. You must remember me, I was famous, you know. No, I can't get you a ticket to that concert. No, you can't use my name, they don't know me anymore. Go figure.

Minor celebrity brought me The Gaze I had spent my life seeking.

After I returned home from London and was working as a national record company publicist, I was offered a job as a radio announcer and found myself thrown into the spotlight. I loved The Gaze that my new-found public persona received and my ego puffed out with pride. Look at me; I am soooo important.

As co-host of a nightly radio show I was inundated with fan mail from pre-teens obsessed with Take That, Boyzone and the Spice Girls. I interviewed International Rock Stars in the privacy of their hotel rooms, dined with movie stars and went to opening nights. Everyone wanted a part of me; the record company representatives who wanted me to play their song, the movie stars who wanted me to promote their film, the TV stars who wanted to be on radio, the boys in the bar who wanted to know someone famous. It was all about me and my ego loved it. I defined myself by my job, ensuring everyone knew who I was, what I did and who I knew.

The next step after radio was television and I lapped up the added attention. My job as a television host brought with it make-up artists, stylists, cameramen, producers and publicists. I had one of each and boy, did I feel important. I rubbed my importance in the face of others less important and watched them seethe. I had the envy I had fought so hard for in the playground.

A job in the spotlight brought with it fabulous parties, celebrity friends, free gym memberships, designer clothes, free drugs, free food, free entry. I dated minor celebrities and got my photo in the paper. I lived in a Sydney waterfront home and thought I had made it. I entered a relationship with a man who drove a convertible, I lived in a house in the right suburb, I had famous friends and money and thought I had found the answer. Rachael Oakes-Ash, radio star. Rachael Oakes-Ash, TV presenter. Rachael Oakes-Ash, girlfriend to the stars. Rachael Oakes-Ash, well-dressed well-toned babe. Rachael Oakes-Ash, she of the sensational house with sensational parties. Rachael Oakes-Ash, she who lives the fabulous lifestyle. Rachael Oakes-Ash, wish I could be like her.

I had thought that the great body, the great job, the great

house, the fabulous man would give me the glamorous lifestyle I believed would save me and make me whole. But when I attained the glamorous lifestyle I had dreamt of I was no different. My thighs still rubbed together in my head, I still gave myself up to my boyfriend of the moment and I competed with other painted talons in the misogynistic world of television. Waking up with a harbour view meant nothing when the man I loved wasn't waking up next to me. Everything that dieting had promised me I had got. I had the man by my side, the glamorous clothes and the invites to parties. But unlike the 'after shots' in the weight loss commercials, I was not smiling.

While songs were playing on the radio I would run to the station fridge and devour promo pies and chocolates. I would ask live on air for pizza and five would arrive within minutes. I kept my weight down with my free gym memberships, free rollerblades and free training sessions. When station politics started affecting my show I would spend my preparation hours in the food hall of the shopping centre next door, munching on fried fish.

I obsessed about my body before I went on camera. Only shoot me from the left, I would say, it's my better side. Is that camera on? I don't want to be shot from behind, you know.

To keep control I sought out naturopaths who put me on organic detox. Now I wandered the food halls munching on dairy-free, wheat-free, egg-free biscuits and obsessed about the milk in my coffee; is it soy?

Then I lost my radio job.

In my post-job blues, at twenty-nine, unemployed and weighing fifty-five kilos, with taut thighs and a flat stomach, I went out to a black tie ball with friends. An off-the-shoulder frock teased the male eyes as I strutted past them. I wanted the attention but I was uncomfortable in my thin body and I drank to obliterate the heat I was attracting. I was lonely but rather than face the loneliness I frantically searched for a toy to distract me. I found him and spent the night in his bed.

When I woke in the arms of this stranger I felt no better or worse; I felt nothing. My need to obliterate myself had meant I had not used any protection the night before. I had refused to take responsibility for my life. I spent the next two weeks wandering like a dazed rabbit, terrified that I had exposed myself to HIV.

I fretted over my behaviour and sought solace in the pantry. I was the thinnest I had been in years but I still could not handle the attention my body was getting.

I sought a blood test in the hope it would be negative and two weeks later it came back positive . . . positively pregnant. My body ballooned with anticipation. I could no longer ignore the consequences of my behaviour. A foetus was developing in my womb. I had thoughts of having children but always pictured a man of my choice by my side. A pregnant body, another two months before an AIDS test would give me the all clear, and a craving for food. This is how I spent my thirtieth birthday.

I booked in for an abortion and awoke from the anaesthetic believing I was nineteen, with the memory of rape, which I had long buried, back in all its graphic glory.

I left my body on the abortion table as I had done on the bonnet of my car. Afterwards I hid in my room with the door closed, curtains drawn, stomach cramps reminding me of the day's events. I spent days calming myself with mashed potato and ice cream, comfort food for a child. Like my rape, I did not dare tell anyone. I was ashamed of my behaviour and its consequences.

The year I turned thirty I lost the symbols by which I defined my persona. My radio gig was already gone. There was no room for me in the new show and I had been shown the door (which my deflated ego had no problem fitting through). Next went the television job when my contract was not renewed. Then my boyfriend dumped me, as a result I lost my position as 'and guest' on the glamorous invitations he received.

Next I lost my sculpted body since without a job I could no longer afford my personal trainers. Then went the designer clothes, for they no longer fitted. I lost my twenties as I turned the milestone thirty. In one year I doubled in size from eight to sixteen. I went from a B-grade celebrity to an office temp in laddered stockings.

No big deal, we've all lost jobs before and I have been dumped by men a thousand times in my short lifetime. I know the speech. 'Chin up, you'll get another job. You'll find somewhere to live. Go on a diet, you'll lose the weight. Sell your designer clothes, they'll pay your rent. Who wants to be twenty-something? Thirty means you're a woman.'

I was left with a series of absences. My home, my job, my relationships, my body and my finances were all in a mess. All my compulsive behaviours went into overdrive, my credit card went through the roof although I had no income to sustain it. I could not stand to be alone with myself and spent hours on the phone tripling my bill. I stole my flatmate's food and gorged in the bathroom.

I had no idea who I was. The lie of my life, that I was a happy, successful, thin, fun-loving individual became fully apparent. I tried dieting and I binged instead. I tried drinking and I woke up more depressed. I tried shopping and ran away in shame when my credit card was rejected. So I tried therapy, making an SOS call in the hope the psychologist's couch could cushion my fall. I managed to return each week and lament my unhappiness.

I rolled in the depression, swam in the depression, relished, savoured and binged on the depression. I hated myself for being depressed; the hate made me more depressed and I would hate myself more.

I was angry at the world, blaming everyone else for my demise. It was my co-host's fault I lost my job, it had nothing to do with my mid-show temper tantrums. It was my flatmate's fault we had to move out, it had nothing to do with the owner wanting to sell. It was their fault I went out, got drunk, was picked up and had an abortion.

The truth was, it was my fault for not standing by myself. In running away from the truth, that I am more than my job, my boyfriend and my home, I had actually abandoned myself. In trying to fill the empty shell I had created a life, a child and risked my life with unprotected sex in the process.

My binges became frantic. Trays of baklava, packets of almond fingers, whole roast chickens and multi-packs of Almond Magnum ice creams bought from the corner store were half-gone before the front door closed behind me. I was used to the frenzy of the bulimic binge but nothing had prepared me for this. There was no desire to purge or to rid myself of this food. I deserved to be fat, slothful and disgusting. I savoured the self-pity and my dishes went unwashed in the sink, my bed stayed unmade and my body began to smell.

Eventually only one skirt, two tops and a pair of underpants were all that still fitted me. I wore them day after day after day. I refused invitations to weddings, parties, to Christmas, to New Year celebrations. Phone calls went unreturned. I hated my friends, I loathed my family, I abhorred my employers. I stared at thin smiling girls and wanted them shot. How could the world smile when I was in such black misery?

I thought of ending it all and began to plan my funeral. Fourteen kilos later I was diagnosed with Binge Eating Disorder and reactive depression. I continued to eat my way through a course of anti-depressants. I talked about the rape in therapy and I ate in the car on the way home. In my depression I remained a child, blaming the world for everything that was wrong.

Few things lifted the blanket of darkness during this time but therapy helped so I increased my sessions to twice a week. I still held onto my depression and my binge eating.

I was addicted to my misery. I could have slept forever, eaten forever and cried forever with a little time left over for ranting, raging, seething and eating some more.

I had been in a similar state before, in London when I was bulimic. But I had structure in my life then; I ate incessantly but I threw up or took laxatives to keep my weight down and I had a gym routine, a work schedule and a relationship, albeit a destructive one. This time I had none of that.

On my thirty-first birthday I took the phone off the hook, rented two videos, bought a family block of chocolate and ordered in Thai food. I had nothing to celebrate. I was caught in a loop. I ate to forget about the rent money I didn't have, I ate to forget about the clothes that didn't fit me so that I couldn't go for a job interview so I couldn't get the money to pay the rent. I ate to forget that the size of my body was preventing me going out. And so on and so on and so on.

Was there a turning point? A specific moment when I realised I had to change? It was more a series of collapses that left me with no options. I was not the smartest of critters at this stage; I waited until all the shit had hit the fan, till everything went wrong before I chose to do anything about it. Choice meant taking responsibility and not blaming everyone else. I gained such pleasure from ranting at the world.

I fed my depression by comparing myself to others. Oh look, she's driving a Saab, I'm not. Oh look, she's married and has a mammoth rock on her finger, I haven't. Oh look, her stomach is so flat and mine is enormous, I am hopeless, unattractive and a failure. The world owes me, I wailed between mouthfuls.

Finally, when I no longer fitted into any of my wardrobe and when I had not showered for four days I realised it was time to stop. The prospect of spending the rest of my life obsessed with my body, refusing invitations out, eating everything in sight, crying into my pillow – a fat, childless, unemployed, lonely spinster with no friends – combined with the realisation that I had already wasted nearly thirty years obsessing about my body and not liking myself very much, meant it was time to change. Time to take responsibility for my own actions, to find a way to change my thoughts and my behaviour.

Of course it does not have to be like that. I was addicted to drama, to suffering and to pain. You don't have to wait until you hit rock bottom to step out of The Gaze, to accept the Average Body and stop believing the Perfect Body will get you the dream life. I have an excessive nature; I live all or nothing and the black-and-white outlook of my life meant my road to recovery would be filled with highs and lows. It's the nature of the game. The high of a binge, the low of the purge.

I made a commitment to myself to find a way out of this weight-obsessed madness but I did not get out of bed straight away and I certainly did not stop over-eating. I made the commitment and then went back to bed. Two steps forward and twelve steps back, that's how I hobbled back home.

12 STEPS, A PAS DE DEUX AND A TRIPLE BACKFLIP

THE DAY I LOST MY JOB as a radio announcer I consulted a psychic over the phone and spent weeks waiting for that offer from Hollywood. I'm still waiting.

I allowed middle-aged men in purple satin to measure the cosmic energy over my body. I burnt Indian herbs on my pressure points. I meditated daily for at least a week. I took up tennis and spent my month's rent on new gear; then I gave it up and took up shopping. I bought a mountain bike but couldn't push it up our hill. I tried cocaine, ecstasy and trips. I tried cocaine again. I became neurotic in my quest to 'find myself' and only succeeded in alienating myself further.

At one stage I was convinced that 'detox' was the answer. The celebrities did it, the magazines told me to do it, and, never one to let a fashion statement pass me by, I did it. I became obsessed with detoxing, believing it would provide me with a cleaner soul, a higher being and a size eight body once again.

If it wasn't detoxing it was shopping; if it wasn't shopping it was hour-long telephone calls or gym classes or drinking parties or health farms, tarot cards or girdles, angel cards, laxatives or Ipecac. I tried weekend rebirthing workshops where we wailed like babies. Anything to change the shape of my body and my world and guarantee my future contentment. I had to go through the entire twelve steps, a pas de deux and a triple backflip before I felt safe in my own body. Travelling the road to recovery from obsessive behaviour is like navigating from an upside-down map at night while keeping one eye on the road. It ain't easy and one wrong turn takes you back to where you started.

STEP ONE: THANK YOUR PARENTS FOR PASSING ON THEIR PROBLEM TO YOU, FORGET THE INITIAL PROBLEM AND CREATE AN OBSESSION

Remember, whatever your parents say they do not realise they have a problem and they certainly don't realise that you have inherited that same problem. In fact, at this stage you don't even realise you have a problem. You are in the embryonic stages of creating and cultivating your own obsession to cover the problem that your parents don't know they gave you.

When cultivating your obsession remember to choose one that will last you for life. Watch your parents, observe them in their own obsessions and then follow suit. If either of your parents is partial to a regular gin and tonic or five then feel free to experiment with the alcohol cabinet. Some obsessions are merely patterns which may not recur until later in life. If, for instance, your mother married a man who was emotionally unavailable, who was constantly away on business or slept around behind her back, then don't expect to emulate this pattern until you are of a sexual age. You may wish to introduce this obsession when you reach Step Six or Eleven.

Play around with the various obsessions on offer and see what suits. For instance, if gambling is more your thing, then don't consider binge eating disorder as you'll have no money to stuff the fridge and might then have to consider anorexia, which is the least fun of all obsessions. Serial adultery was popular in the past but with the onslaught of sexually transmitted diseases it has lost some of its appeal so if you choose this one then take out shares with Durex.

Remember there are plenty of obsessions to go around and psychologists are discovering new disorders daily. Whatever you choose, have fun cultivating it since this will probably be the last time you gain true enjoyment from your obsession. It will soon become a daily, weekly or monthly ritual played out to keep your life from falling apart.

STEP TWO: CULTIVATE THE OBSESSION YOU HAVE CREATED TO FORGET THE INITIAL PROBLEM PASSED ON BY YOUR PARENTS

Before an obsession can become an obsession you must practise it daily. It takes time and effort to create a good obsession. If it's food, then see how many Iced Vovo buscuits you can eat in one sitting. Start with ten and work your way up to a packet. Try semi-frozen cakes before moving on to the deep freeze and always try to turn to your obsession whenever you feel uncomfortable or upset since this helps the obsession to take hold.

Keep a list of obsessions by your phone or next to your bed. When you wake from a disturbing dream or hang up from a call to your mother or your ex-boyfriend scan the list of obsessions you are choosing from and go with what works for you. If your dream woke you at 2 a.m. then the light of the fridge door may illuminate your problem. If your mother called mid-morning then a lunchtime shopping frenzy should soothe those worry lines. If something is troubling you at work hold off until the end of the day when the bar is open. You can always ring ahead and reserve your favourite bar stool.

STEP THREE: DENY THE OBSESSION CREATED TO FORGET THE PROBLEM

This step is often the hardest to acknowledge, because why

would you knowingly deny an obsession you now realise you don't have? (If you know what I mean.) But if you have cultivated your obsession well, then it will come naturally.

STEP FOUR: ACKNOWLEDGE THE OBSESSION AND ADD TWO MORE

Your credit card bill, bathroom scales, and Pap smear test will usually have alerted you to your obsession by now. At this stage it is best to acknowledge that you may have to cut back on your obsession. If there are any other obsessions that you are drawn to, introduce them now. They will act as a decoy to the original obsession and will help you to achieve Step Five.

STEP FIVE: FORGET THE ACKNOWLEDGEMENT OF THE OBSESSION AND ASK WHAT PROBLEM?

As you ignore the initial obsession in your cultivation of the two new obsessions you will also forget that you may have acknowledged the first obsession. You may, in a moment of panic, have confided your obsession, which will be seen as the problem, to one or two of your closest friends, your hairdresser or a door-to-door salesman. When they bring it up again deny it, ask 'what problem?' and then proudly show off your new obsessions.

STEP SIX: VAGUELY ACKNOWLEDGE THAT YOU ACKNOWLEDGED THE OBSESSION BUT VOW TO FORGET IT AND CREATE ANOTHER OBSESSION TO HELP YOU FORGET THE FORGOTTEN PROBLEM

You may be forced, unknowingly, into acknowledging that you acknowledged the original obsession. This is good; it means you have progressed to Step Six. For instance, if your obsession was compulsive spending then you may receive a phone call from your credit manager regarding the payment which is now three months overdue. At this stage you have to acknowledge your obsession but don't fret, simply agree with the bank manager, send him a dud cheque to keep him quiet, put the credit card statement under your bed with all the parking fines and reach for a Mogodon, martini or mud cake or refer to the list by your phone.

STEP SEVEN: UNDER EXTREME DURESS, ACKNOWLEDGE THE ORIGINAL OBSESSION AGAIN

Note that Step Seven is always performed under extreme duress. You may be late for a job interview because you can no longer squeeze into your size ten interview suit, you may have killed the dog as you reversed down the driveway after your Weetbix and vodka, or you may be fending off the debt collectors by impersonating a rottweiler from behind your front door. Whatever the crisis, an immediate acknowledgement of your obsession is required to move onto Step Eight.

STEP EIGHT: VOW TO DO SOMETHING ABOUT THE OBSESSION, REMEMBERING WHICH OBSESSION YOU ARE VOWING TO DO SOMETHING ABOUT

It is important when experiencing Step Eight that you remember which was your original obsession as it is this obsession that you are vowing to do something about. Don't freak out; remember, if you have completed all the steps you should have a spare two or three extra obsessions to fall back on. Also remember, vowing to do something about it doesn't always mean doing something about it.

If you are a binge eater you may vow to go on a diet. You may only last a day but at least you have vowed. If you are an alcoholic you may vow to have a single malt whisky instead of a double. If you are obsessed with your ex-boyfriend you may vow only to call him three times today instead of five hundred. At this stage it is the vow that is most important, the hard part comes with Step Nine.

STEP NINE: TREAT THE OBSESSION (BUT NOT THE PROBLEM BECAUSE YOU DON'T REMEMBER YOU HAD A PROBLEM TO START WITH)

Now you have acknowledged you have an obsession you need to start controlling it. If you are an alcoholic you may cut back from spirits to beer and then from beer to table vinegar. If you are a smoker you may decide to roll your joints straight and without cigarette tobacco. If you are a binge eater or chronic dieter and obsessed with your body you may control your obsession by eating three healthy meals a day and continue to do this for some weeks. The more you commit to controlling your obsession the bigger the high you get from the obsession control, the tighter the restrictions. The added bonus in Step Nine is that the treatment of the obsession can lead to an extra obsession itself.

STEP TEN: BELIEVE YOU ARE CURED

After a few hours without alcohol, a week without spending and the loss of five kilos you will then embark upon Step Ten, believing you are cured. This is the shortest step in the program.

STEP ELEVEN: ACKNOWLEDGE THE RETURN OF THE OBSESSION AND THE TWO NEW ONES THAT REPLACED IT

As your thighs push against the seams of your new size six gym shorts, as the commission-based sales assistants start calling you at home, as your flatmate's Tim Tams mysteriously disappear and the packets are found under your bed, you may be forced to acknowledge the return of your obsession, but only for a moment because by now you should be well into the two new obsessions that slipped in to replace the original obsession during the time you thought you were cured.

STEP TWELVE: SEEK PROFESSIONAL HELP

If you have followed the program step by step then you

should now have more obsessions than either of your parents started with. You may find that juggling them all is more difficult than you thought. You wake up at 5 a.m. to maintain your exercise obsession with a five kilometre jog followed by a quick shower and a scrub of the shower tiles, where you have noticed mould has appeared since yesterday's anal retentive pre-work spring clean. You finish your breakfast of half a lettuce leaf and spring water, feeling thin and pure, before you drive to work, stopping at the servo on the way for a Magnum, Mars Bar and meat pie.

As you settle in at your desk you automatically reach for the hip flask in your third drawer before ringing your ex-boyfriend's new girlfriend's number and hanging up. By mid-morning you can't take it anymore and buy the latest see-through vacuum cleaner in bright colours so you can watch the dirt in your life being sucked away along with this month's rent. While you're out you pick up two new lipsticks, a CD that will look good on your shelf but you'll never listen to and a bag of kitty litter in case you buy a cat sometime in the near future.

You return to work, hiding behind the water cooler when you spot your credit manager waiting in your office, making a detour through the staff kitchen, grabbing the office junior's three sandwiches and someone's left-over casserole from the fridge on the way. A spew session in the toilet is followed by another call to the ex-boyfriend's new girlfriend and then a call to your coke dealer for an extra gram. Call the psychic hot line and spend $300 listening to your recorded future, ask your assistant to screen your calls lest your bank manager persists and then get onto the Internet for a quick game of BlackJack.

On the way home you pick up a carton of Benson and Hedges and three packets of Tally Ho cigarette papers. After decoding the three alarms and unlocking two deadlocks you enter your house and check your fax, emails, pager and answering machine before cleaning the toilet bowl. You choose a dusk-pink towel from the colour-coded linen closet, taking care to square away the white towels lined up against the off-white and the ivory. After a twenty-minute shower you wash your hands ten times before checking your emails again and relaxing with a joint. Seven minutes before retiring, having taken a Normison to help you sleep, an Alka Seltzer for your stomach and vitamins B through to E, you lay your runners and gym gear out at the foot of the bed for the morning, call the tarot line for tomorrow's prediction and call your ex-boyfriend's new girlfriend one more time before passing out.

It's now time to seek professional help. At this point, do not give in to your New Age obsession with all things spiritual as a form of recovery. By the time you reach Step Twelve you need immediate and qualified help. Seek out a counsellor and transfer all your obsessions onto him/her as you prepare to Pas se Deux.

PAS DE DEUX: AS YOU SEE THE LIGHT YOU DEVELOP AN UNCANNY ABILITY TO SEE EVERYBODY ELSE'S SHIT – NOW TELL THEM ALL ABOUT IT

After three months of therapy you have developed a sixth sense and can now see everybody else's shit clearly. You proceed to inform your mother of her martyr obsession, you tell your father that he needs to deal with his control issues and inform your boss that some childhood regression therapy should fix that power problem he's got. You're convinced your best mate is experiencing penis envy and proceed to tell her so in the middle of the next dinner party, and you feel it's only fair to let your ex-boyfriend know that his fixation with his mother is unhealthy. Having fixed the world you can't understand why no one is returning your calls.

SINGLE BACKFLIP: BREAK DOWN WHEN YOU REALISE EVERYBODY ELSE'S SHIT IS REALLY YOUR OWN SHIT

You'll know you've completed the Pas de Deux when you are no longer invited home for Christmas, your best friend has switched to a silent number without telling you, your boss has been transferred to another department and your ex-boyfriend's mother is sending you hate mail. It's time to look in the mirror and backflip.

DOUBLE BACKFLIP: START CLEANING UP YOUR OWN SHIT AND FORGET ABOUT EVERYONE ELSE'S

The Double Backflip is the longest step in the whole program. It involves complete self-obsession. You may have to withdraw from the world in order to gain the momentum to complete it. The Double Backflip is all about getting back to the problem. Remember the problem? It was way back in Step One and in order to get to the problem you're going to have to work backwards through all the steps one by one until you reach the problem you have forgotten – get it? If you don't, you may have to employ a professional backflipper to help you flip back through your past to get to the forgotten problem. Or you may join a group of backflippers and compare notes each week on the progress of each other's backflips. Of course, a backflip should never be performed without appropriate support – a cushion to break the falls which will inevitably happen. Only then will you be ready to complete the Triple Backflip.

TRIPLE BACKFLIP: GET OVER IT

Congratulations! You are either now a healthy happy individual or you are six foot under. This all depends on how long it took you to get to this final stage of the process.

MUTINY IN AISLE SIX

IT HAPPENED IN AISLE SIX. It had been a bitch of a day.

The zip on my Lycra denim hipsters had broken in the morning struggle. The front page of the newspaper heralded the resurgence of the waif model with full colour photos. My car mirror magnified the sugar zit on my forehead and inside the supermarket my now-famous ex-schoolfriend was plastered across the weekly tabloids in her wedding dress, looking every bit the beaming thin movie star that she was.

I experienced a major trolley jam in the Tim Tam aisle (they would be on special), there was a spillage in aisle five which prevented me from nabbing the bagels and running, I peered deep into frozen foods to hide from an old gym friend and I wondered how many more times I could visit the free sausage tasting in the meat section before I had to buy something.

I perused the shelves adorned on one side with no-fat-no-sugar-no-dairy hot chocolate, and on the other with custard-filled brioche hot from the oven. One aisle offered me diet soda, laxatives and protein shakes. The next tempted me with Belgian white chocolate mingled with nuts. Girls in tight Lycra whizzed past me with trolleys full of fruit. Women with five children balanced on each hip and dark rings circling their zombied eyes were pushing mountains of sugar from aisle to aisle.

My shoulders began to throb, my teeth were grinding and a light sweat was steaming off me. I filled my trolley with carrots, cardboard disguised as crispbread, saccharine ice cream, skimmed milk and cereal fibre. I longed for Haagen Daaz, shortbread, Brie and Swiss cheese, chocolate milk and Froot Loops cereal.

By the time I made it to aisle six I was an overcooked pumpkin ready to explode.

Stop this supermarket, I screamed, I want to get off.

In a frenzy I hijacked another shopper's trolley already filled with forbidden food and began to pillage the shelves, stocking up on ammo – three tubs of full-cream vanilla bean, twelve warm doughnuts sparkling with cinnamon, sugar-coated muesli. I was ready to do battle with every Lycra-clad stick-figured gym instructor, dietitian, food analyst and TV commercial that told me that fat girls don't get lucky, fat girls don't look good, fat girls are spinsters. I was ready to engage in war with every half-baked-low-fat-low-fibre-low-sugar-low-life diet food on the market.

I burnt rubber in Woolworths that day (you can still see the skid marks in the biscuit aisle) and a new woman was born in aisle six.

Ever felt like that? Wanted to tell the whole diet world to get stuffed? Wanted to scream to the world, 'I am fat; have you got a problem with that?' Wanted to tell those thin little wenches with their lettuce-filled shopping bags to get their eyes out of your trolley and their mouths into the fridge?

I have. After more than twenty years of dieting it finally occurred to me that day in aisle six that diets simply don't work. If they did, why was I still doing it? I had trusted Dr Scarsdale, Dr Cabot, the entire Israeli Army, the Pritikin centre, Jenny Craig, Gloria Marshall and Weight Watchers and I felt let down. Thirty years of paper-thin crackers and weekly weigh-ins, of cellulite cream, sweat pants and mid-morning cravings.

I knew diets weren't working. I was forever trapped in the gym when I wanted to be outside in the sun, simply because I was petrified what getting off the aerobic cycle would mean. My life was held together by the promise of a new body when I didn't even know the old one. If life got too tough I could always go on a diet and then I'd get the new job and the hot man for sure. It never happened. I was buying on credit that day in aisle six, out of work and single.

Dieting had taught me that good girls are thin and that sex is naughty and powerful. I learnt that my thin body held magical powers with devastating consequences. If sex is bad and being thin is good then why do only good girls get sex? I asked. I thought it must be a double sin to be both fat and sexual. To be fat and sexual was just plain greedy.

But the alternative was frightening. Stopping dieting held too harsh consequences. My fears were numerous . . . If I stop dieting I'll be the size of a house . . . I'm already the size of a house . . . my hunger needs to be kept in check: if I let it out it will devour everything . . . I like dieting: it gives me an illusion of control . . .

When I lost everything that I had defined myself by I realised my life had become unmanageable and that my eating had prevented me from achieving many goals. I had used my imagined fat as a reason why I should not apply for jobs I thought would go to the thin girl and why I did not deserve a healthy relationship. Subconsciously I knew I was using food to prevent me from moving ahead, growing up and becoming an adult. That's why I binged. I blamed my body for my dire straits and I used food to soften the blow.

In order for me to stop the bingeing I had to take my power back, stop blaming the food and start accepting my own choice to eat. I had to become present when food was in front of me. I had to stop endowing it with emotional qualities. The food didn't hate me, the food didn't love me; it didn't invite me to eat it; it had no thoughts about me and no emotional investment in whether I chose to eat it or not. It was simply food – but try telling that to a woman with a body issue problem.

The daily cycle of bingeing starts with an agitation, a niggling under the skin, a bad taste in the mouth or the feel of your thighs rubbing together. That's what scientists call the Butterfly Effect: the theory that a butterfly's wings flapping in the Amazon may have profound effects somewhere else. A tiny movement, a small change can build into a mammoth event.

Binge triggers are so subtle that often the binger has no idea where it started. A mother's phone call, a bill received in the post, the scratching of Lycra against the stomach, even a glance from a girlfriend over coffee can often escalate into a full-blown binge disaster five hours or five days later. If the binger knew the trigger then they'd be halfway to choosing not to binge but in the throes of binge behaviour the butterfly wings go unheeded.

The uneasy feeling builds up as the day progresses and the number of stresses increases until the binger is thinking of nothing but food. She starts with a nibble from the kitchen, perhaps a bite of toast or last night's leftovers or a stale biscuit left over from last week's dinner party. The resolve is now broken and shelves are upturned for baked beans, chocolate sauce, Ryvitas, Weetbix and porridge – anything to make the uneasiness go away.

Ten minutes, maybe twenty, later and she's repulsed by the carnage in the kitchen and obsessed by the extra layer of fat that has mysteriously appeared on her hips. The second stage of the binge cycle begins.

Must get rid of this fat, must get rid of this fat, can't let it fester, must get rid of this fat. Some women will then recreate the kitchen cupboard carnage in the bathroom, searching for Alka Seltzer, Epsom Salts, laxatives – and swallow the lot. Others will stick their fingers down their throats or tickle their tonsils with toothbrushes while hunched over the toilet bowl. For some just bending the body over will create a projectile hurl. Others don their Nikes and run a marathon around the neighbourhood. The purge lasts until something else triggers another binge and the cycle continues.

The high-powered banker may enjoy a three-hour pissy lunch complete with a six-hundred dollar bottle of dessert wine simply because his wife called at 11 a.m. and nagged him about fixing the roof of the holiday house. The checkout chick spends her electricity payment on a new pair of shoes because her boyfriend dumped her the night before. The plumber nips down the bookie's during smoko and blows his month's alimony payment on a horse called Dream Away Out because his boss took his own marital problems out on him that morning and now all the plumber can think of is his alcoholic father, six feet under.

The banker does not acknowledge that his wife's nagging makes him feel inadequate, that why he works such long hours and drives a BMW is because he is still trying to prove to his own father that he is good enough, rich enough, big enough. So he reacts by taking a well-earned break, only he turns it into a three hour drinking-and-spending marathon.

The checkout chick doesn't understand that the new shoes aren't going to take away the pain. All she knows is that when she buys a new pair of shoes she feels sexy and when she feels sexy she can get laid on a Saturday night and that even if she does wake up on Sunday morning with some strange guy's pubic hairs on her sheets at least she wasn't alone.

The tradesman knows he's a failure, his dad told him all his life, his boss told him this morning and the TAB proved it when Dream Away Out ran the race backwards. He's compelled to prove it over and over again. And for those moments when Dream Away Out breaks into the race, for those seconds in his life he's a winner.

Bingeing is an expensive process and often money issues and body issues go hand in hand. When you have such little respect for your body then you're hardly going to have a healthy respect for your bank balance. Living hand to mouth takes on a whole new meaning for the bulimic.

Just like food, money has always been an issue. When I got it, I spent it, purging it excessively until it was all gone and I was in debt again.

Naturally, I saw no reason why lack of funds should prevent me from living the life I aspired to. So I would steal my father's Cabcharge card and bribe cabbies to write out fake dockets for trips never made, keeping twenty dollars for themselves and giving forty to me. The guilt kept me in the cycle of excess. To appease the guilt I would overcompensate for my extreme behaviour by setting limits on myself. Like my eating, my limits in themselves were excessive. No eating or spending for a week, and then I'd binge.

The truth is I could not just stop at one. Sales assistants loved me. 'Of course, the cleansing lotion won't work unless you have the toner, the moisturiser, the anti-ageing eye cream, face mask and exfoliator.' I understood that there was simply no point in purchasing one item when I could purchase the whole range. I also understood that if I was to go to the gym then I must go daily, twice a day if I could, that the occasional gym workout meant nothing as you may as well just stay home.

Hence I purchased gym memberships and went overboard for a month before spending the next eleven months on my arse at home. Similarly it would be rude to stop at the one drink. If I was drinking then I was getting drunk, what other point was there to alcohol? If I had a credit card then I must reach its limit or not have one at all. If I'm taking up tennis then I must have the tennis racket, tennis skirt, little white socks and tennis shoes or not bother. If I was offered more I'd always say yes. Yes, yes, yes, oooooh yes!

So just what compels us to purchase life-changing products that sit unopened on our bathroom shelves and behind our garage doors?

Pain, P-A-I-N, pain with a capital P, a long drawn out A, a silent but all-consuming I and an N to top it all off. Got to keep busy or the pain will get you, got to keep running or it'll tap you on your back. Got to keep buying, spending; buy, buy, buy or the pain will rear its familiar head.

Me, running from pain, you say? What have I got to be in pain about you ask as you check your emails again, ring home for the third time this hour to check your messages and pour your fifth cup of coffee. It's a lonely old world out there if we just stop. If we stop, sit and be silent. The illusion of a full life and a full diary almost fools us that we are not empty and alone.

Portfolios, shares, property, bonds, futures, options are the current compulsion of city dwellers desperate to achieve immortality. Don't be left behind, keep up with the double-barrelled names next door. Drive European, eat Asian, wear French underwear, Italian outerwear and Swiss metal wear. Drink Russian, exercise American, holiday African. Know a celebrity, spot a celebrity, touch a celebrity, kill your wife and become a celebrity.

I am exhausted just thinking about it; I need a good lie down and a packet of Tim Tams, or maybe I'll go on a three day run.

Yes, I believed I could have it all and did not understand the consequences of such thinking. Yes, I was a glutton for punishment and yes, I thrived on the self-flagellation. 'The bank manager's on the phone again. I am so hopeless, I spent three hundred dollars on that gym membership and haven't been once. I am a fat pig. I got so drunk last night and called people names, I am such a disgusting bitch.' To understand this excessive behaviour I would have to accept that no one is perfect, stop spending so much time with my head in the toilet, the fridge and the bottle in an attempt to hide my imperfections, to avoid seeing just where I was lacking.

Of course after the binge, be it eating, or spending, or taking drugs and drinking so as not to think about food, I knew I was no good. I could not fool myself that I was perfect. There were only two ways to exist, perfect and best or hideous and the bottom of the worst. Black or white, all or nothing, no in between. Moderation was boring. It was for grown-ups, adults and school prefects. I preferred the peak of the binge followed by the trough of the purge. I was always travelling too fast on the way up or down to pause mid-way and take a look around.

My desire was to have it all and I could not cope when I didn't get it. As the youngest of three girls I considered myself the princess and if my parents never said no, how could anyone else? If I can't have the best twenty-first birthday party in the world then I won't have one at all. I have cut off my nose to spite my face so many times. I am surprised I have any nose left. Some would call me a spoilt brat but I preferred to think of myself as hard-done-by.

My illimitable behaviour was often mistaken for insubordination as I tussled with my immediate superiors in the workplace. My ears were deaf to 'no' and automatically replaced it with 'yes'. This created a few problems for my career. While working in restaurants in London my extreme behaviour did not go unnoticed. I would ignore the pleas from my boss to toe the line and listen to what she had to say. Instead I made up my own rules and pushed what limits there were out of the way.

When the managing director called me into his office and asked me to leave, I was shocked and appalled. I could not understand why he would do such a thing and became convinced it was his problem not mine. Humiliated, I told anyone who would listen what a mean and nasty man he was. He must be a misogynist, I would wail to any strangers within spitting distance. You know he's got his hand in the till, don't you? The accompanying guilt at annihilating this innocent man would set me up for another binge and the Cycle of Self-Loathing would continue.

When boyfriends said no my gluttony would manifest itself in self-starvation. 'You're dropped' . . . the ultimate limit! I could not cope with this one. As man after man dared to say no I wallowed in my misery on the Stairmaster. I pounded my frustration on the aerobic floor and I refused to let a morsel pass my lips. Fuck you, fuck you, fuck you, I would say – but to whom, him or me?

While gluttony for punishment prevented me from acknowledging any confines placed on me it also left me mute to setting boundaries with others. I could not hear 'no' and I could not say 'no' either. Drinks on Friday night; you'll be there, won't you, Rach? *Yes*. Hey, Rach, it's Sal, having dinner at my house Friday night, would love to see you! *Sure, what time?* I've got tickets to see Alanis on Friday night and I immediately thought of you, shall I count you in? *Yes, please*. Friday night would then be spent head in ice-cream bucket while my answering machine flashed with messages from all the friends I had made promises to, demanding to know where I was. They'd hate me for a few days, but not as long as I would hate myself.

My inability to say no often meant I would resent the people I said yes to. You don't mind if I borrow your favourite party dress for the night and return it ripped and dirty, do you, Rach? *No problem*. I am feeling dreadful, I know you broke up with your boyfriend last night, Rach, but I really feel so depressed and in need of a good cry, can I come round for a coffee? *The kettle's on*. I've put you down for a Nutri-metics party, I knew you'd do it, you've got such a great place and it's only eight girls and it'll be so much fun, it's this Wednesday, you don't mind cancelling your yoga class, do you? *Why make it only eight?* Invite more. I simply couldn't set a limit on my friends' behaviour for fear they would no longer like me, so I said yes and hated them instead.

Okay, okay, so let's say we just stop. Stop running and turn around and face whatever it is we're running from. What then? Personally, I know I would have saved a fortune in credit card bills, been seven kilos lighter and my phone bill would have been cut in half. I would also have been scared. The times when I did stop running I had to explain to myself why I hated myself so much, then I had to put myself in my shoes. How do I like it when I keep running from me? How would I like it if I never listened to myself or truly heard myself? How do I like it when I treat myself as if I don't exist?

I wrote lists of all the wonderful things in my life I had to be thankful for. My pad remained empty the first week. I kept going. I overdosed on self-help books. *You're a Winner, They're a Winner, I am a Healthy Happy Venetian with No Need to go to Mars, Please Stop Me, I'm Competing Myself to Death.* I looked at my life instead of looking at everyone else's and then I looked away again. I searched for a support group, Competitors Anonymous, and attended a meeting. I arrived first, spoke loudest and longest, contributed the most money and was the last to leave. I was asked not to return.

I was missing something. I had a house wallpapered with affirmations and a self-help library Oprah would die for and I still found myself busting to tell the better story at lunch, in the office, at the gym. 'Anything I can do I can do better, I can do anything better than me!' I was competing with the world and with myself and in order to stop one of me had to step out of the game. So which one would it be? Child Rach with her Patented Five Step Plan to Getting What She Wants? Or Diet-Master Rach with her 'I Must Control You and All That You Eat' attitude? Or Binge Pal Rach with her 'No One Else is as Out of Control as Me' drive?

I once thought that staying home would stop me competing with others. I locked myself away, believing if I physically removed myself from the public arena then it would stop. Instead I found myself competing with Elle, Naomi and Claudia as I flicked through the pages of my magazines. So I threw the magazines out. I screamed at the television, searching for a spare piece of meat, a bulge, a sagging boob, a fault on the bodies of the prime-time princesses. So I turned the television off. I read books from my shelf and told myself I was more in control than Bridget Jones before burning the book in my bath while eating a packet of marshmallows.

I called my sister and compared bank accounts and lives. She won. So I pulled out the phone. I sat at the window and watched my neighbours go to work. I guessed the designer labels on their back and gloated in my superior wardrobe. So I closed the curtains. I looked in the mirror and did not like what I saw. So I took down all the mirrors and turned them against the wall. To get away I went to bed, only to dream of boyfriend-stealing girls who were prettier than me. Competition with other women was such a mammoth part of my life that it was going on twenty-four hours a day, even in my sleep.

I didn't have to face my own flesh and hunger for excess as long as there was always someone fatter than me, poorer than me, more dysfunctional than me. By comparison, then, I was perfect. I am the first to admit I didn't feel comfortable at a party until I could spot someone a size larger than me. I would scan the room with my fat-girl radar until I hit a target and then I would breathe easy and take pity on the poor fat girl in the corner, which could so easily have been me if the poor fat girl had decided to stay home with Haagen Daaz for the night.

Should there be no fatter woman at the party; should my worst nightmare have come true and I found myself surrounded by a sea of Courtneys, Jennifers and Calistas then I had no choice but to make up for my body size, to overcompensate for my extra flesh and apologise for taking up more than my allotted space. This usually involved mixing pints of vodka with Sambuca shots and as the nectar washed over me my flesh disappeared, my voice got louder and my attention-beacon brighter.

I figured there must be other options short of locking myself away. I went out and vowed to walk away when I felt myself competing. I spent a lot of time walking. I became obsessed with affirmations, covering my dashboard, my computer, the back of my door, my bathroom mirror, my fridge, my television with 'I am enough, I am enough, I am enough'. I smiled when my friends got a new job, a new car, a new house. I refrained from commenting about weight loss or weight gain and kept yellow Post-it notes by the phone to remind myself 'I speak positively of all people', but I still had a long long way to go before I could give up the dieting for good.

LEAVE THE LIGHT ON IN THE FRIDGE

FOUR YEARS AND TWELVE STEPS after my London confession it was time to turn the light on in the fridge and take a look at what it showed.

I had lived a life of general excess – a wardrobe in three different sizes, a reserved spot on the Stairmaster at the gym and a premium customer discount at the local bakery. I had lost jobs due to my excess and had ruined relationships because of my self-loathing. Enough was enough.

It's just the kind of gal I am. A ferocious devourer of anything and everything. I have 'mouth hunger' daily when my eyes grow bigger than my stomach. I want the holiday in Mauritius I see in the newspaper, the shoes in the shop window, the car pulled up next to me at the lights. Anything that will enhance my image I want. Now I only want it for a second, but before I could obsess about it for hours. Other women obsess about relationships and getting married, or buying a home, or their ex-boyfriend's new girlfriend. Some women are content with what they have and are not tempted by the seductive images presented to them in the paper, shop catalogues and shop windows. I could never be one of those women.

In my desire to understand my compulsive eating I began

to research the methods available to me to stop my bingeing. I became as obsessive about my recovery as I had been about my bingeing, overloading on books and courses as if they were an all-you-can-eat banquet. I opened an account at Amazon and gorged on self-help books: *How to Stop Bingeing in Eight Easy Minutes; You are Not What you Eat; Help, I'm in the Fridge.* I surfed the net and met up with like-minded bingers trying to tackle their obsession. The Internet truly is an excellent resource for eating-disordered persons. It is private and you do not have to risk exposing yourself until you are ready.

I learnt that I had to accept my body in all its rippled glory first, and struggled with this daily for months. I thought about throwing out all my thin clothes and then I thought about it some more. Eventually I moved them from my wardrobe and piled them into the blanket box: out of sight, out of mind. I was no longer reminded by my closet each day what a fat out-of-control thing I was. The empty hanging space was filled with new clothes that fitted my present size. When shopping for these clothes I reminded myself that nobody looks good in fluorescent cheap lighting and that dressing room mirrors are bought at a bulk discount from the circus. I removed my own full-length mirrors and found I no longer obsessed every minute about how I looked.

I discovered the work of Geneen Roth, the leader of the no-diet movement in America. It terrified me. Stop dieting, she encouraged. Diets don't work, she reassured me from the pages of her book. I knew that, I was walking proof they don't work, but I was too terrified to stop. If I stopped, then I gave up hope. Hope that the perfect body exists, hope that I'll find the perfect life if I find the perfect body, and hope that the perfect body will grant me immortality and I'll live forever, wrinkle-free.

I put my eating habits under the microscope, examining what I was doing when I chose to eat, realising when I ate for hunger and when I ate for comfort. I took the food out of the fridge, put it on a plate and ate it in full view of my flatmate, my parents, my friends and my workmates. I acknowledged my terror in doing this and did it all the same.

Geneen's books told me to fill my cupboards with food, bring all that was previously illegal into the kitchen pantry and stock up. When you eat a packet of biscuits, replace it with another. Surround yourself with food and eat every time you are hungry.

I imagined drowning in a sea of caramel sauce, my bloated carcass bobbing on the surface, the Fire Department breaking down my door and hosing me down before winching me by crane to the morgue. A kitchen filled with never-ending Tim Tams, ice cream, chicken-and-leek pies, mashed potato, rice pudding and taramasalata would be heaven or hell, depending on my mood at the time. A kitchen filled with food could never be simply a kitchen filled with food. I had a fridge, I had a pantry but the shelves were always empty and now I was being asked to fill it . . . aaaah!

After twenty-odd years of eating in private, to step out and show my hunger to the world, to say 'I am hungry and I deserve to eat' was sheer terror. A thousand thoughts roamed my head. 'If I eat in public they'll know I'm bulimic'. 'If I eat I'll get fat'. 'If I bring chocolate into my house it will last two seconds'. 'If my fridge is full people will think I'm a glutton'. 'I won't fit into my clothes'. 'I can't do this, I have no resolve'. 'God, I can't stop eating'.

I left the light on in the fridge whenever I ate, even if I was bingeing, and I allowed myself to binge when I knew no other way to deal with whatever had happened earlier to set me off. When my friends wanted to diet I politely declined. I longed to fix myself with a diet but I knew it would only be temporary.

No binge is better or worse, and whether I stole from old

people, Year Nine students or from the work fridge, the result was still the same – self-loathing. If I remained a binger I could always blame something else for my pain but if I remained a binger I remained a child and at thirty-one years of age it was time I grew up and became empowered by my own responsible choices. My rebellious inner child thought it sounded boring as bat shit.

No matter how often I binged I would never be the three-year-old on the trike again. No amount of bingeing and purging would bring my dad home from his interstate business trips or make my mum Carol Brady or make me the centre of everyone else's universe.

I was surprised one day when I noticed a half-finished tub of Sara Lee in my freezer. It had been there for months. I was more surprised when I started throwing away food which had gone uneaten. I was still more surprised when my body craved vegetables, salads and legumes and enjoyed them. Imagine my delight when my body began to shrink and slowly return to its natural size. This delight was often short-lived, for the moment I rejoiced at weight loss my head entered diet territory and I rebelled with a series of binges.

If something went wrong, dieting would fix it. If I could not control my outside world and the people in it then I could control my body. To give up dieting meant growing up, stepping out into the fridge light and facing my demons. Letting go of the dream of 'when I am thin'. It was much easier to blame the outside world for my woes. It's my mother's fault, my boss's fault, my co-host's fault, my sister's fault, my flatmate's fault, the fault of the man who punctures the Sara Lee pies with fork prongs.

Two steps forward and one step back, that's how my body reacted. Weight loss and the perfect body were not the goal, eating when hungry was not a diet program, eating when hungry is what normal people do. Losing weight was merely a byproduct of establishing a normal, healthy and natural relationship with food. I had to understand this, accept this, and really want it in order to stop the bingeing backlash that weight loss always brought with it.

I was holding onto my fat because I was afraid of change. I knew I could not diet again, I was terrified of remaining fat but I was just as terrified of trusting that my body would drop to its natural weight.

No matter how I avoided it I knew the emotional work had to be done if I was ever to break free from my rigid thought patterns. This took work. I kept a food diary and also recorded the events that happened before I ate. After six weeks patterns began to emerge. Surprise, surprise . . . I ate to swallow anger when I didn't stand up for myself. I ate when I swallowed what my boss said even though I disagreed. I ate when I said yes when I meant no. I began to realise the kind of changes that had to be made.

If I wanted to grow up I would have to learn how to hear and say 'no'. I would also have to learn how to play nicely with the others and decide which playmates were bad news. Growing up is about setting limits. I became my own parent and wrestled with my child Rach, who didn't want to budge. The alternatives were to continue my unlimited actions until I was wanted by the worldwide credit force or sit at home and eat until I was given my own postcode.

I had to learn to say 'no' in order to interrupt my inexhaustible desire to binge on every compulsion I could find.

Like many women, I rebelled against the limits the grown-up world places on us by being limitless with sex, shopping, alcohol and food. Relationships have crumbled because my ears were 'no'-deficient and my boyfriends didn't respond to the silent treatment, the barrage of abuse, the pleading, the blackmail or the sugar-coated compliments. Jobs have been lost (I have often mistaken the workplace for kindergarten and behaved accordingly, right down to hogging the water fountain), bank balances shattered (try explaining to the bank manager why you couldn't take 'no' for an answer when presented with a $300 pair of shoes and only $10 in the bank), chins tripled (food never responds to the silent treatment), Saturdays vanished in post-alcoholic daze, friends scorned and landlords ignored because I refused to hear the word 'no'. There's something very unappealing about a grown woman throwing a tantrum.

Without rules, laws and restrictions there is anarchy. When we live as five-year-olds with foolhardy five-step plans in a grown-up world we don't last long. When we are not declaring anarchy in the workforce (filing the T's under the B's and shredding the contents of our boss's in-tray, or spiking our boss's coffee with full cream instead of skimmed milk and sugar instead of Nutra-sweet) then we declare anarchy on our bodies. We want it all and our mothers never told us we could not have it, for they hoped for it themselves.

Of course, being an extremist meant I took to saying 'no' with a little too much enthusiasm. No, I cried, No, No, No. Rach, would you like to come shopping with me while I choose some paints for the new house I have bought with all of my masses of money which you don't have? No, I would rather not, I said and then suffered a 'no' hangover for two days. I couldn't sleep because of the anxiety I felt that my friend would not ask me out again.

Would you work this Saturday night for me, Rach? No, I said. Oh, go on, Rach, my grandmother is dying and my pet frog has pneumonia. No, I can't, I said, and stamped my foot.

I went from a people-pleasing sap to a wall of concrete overnight. Carried away with my newfound vocabulary, I said no to everything until I realised my phone no longer rang and my doorbell was dusty. I had spent my life saying yes to everyone when I really meant no. I had said yes because I wanted to be liked, and inevitably ended up letting them down when I didn't show. Saying no was a terrifying experience. The sky would fall in if I said no. People would see me for the vile, hideous, disgusting creature I really was, and they wouldn't invite me out again. If I don't say yes to the job then there is no other opportunity. My sister will never speak to me again if I say no. It's hard to let go of thirty-odd years of all-or-nothing thinking.

Saying no was about satisfying my own needs and now I really felt like the self-centred, self-obsessed git I had always accused myself of being. My friendships went under the microscope. Friends could be classified into two categories, excessive and destructive or meek and mild. Once again, there was no in-between. My extreme gesture was to cut the destructive out of my life: those friends that I felt compelled to be excessive with, to binge drink, binge eat and binge gossip with.

The meek and mild were finally given the chance to speak up and those who stood up to me stayed. The friends who never took no for an answer, who emotionally blackmailed me, competed with me, said they'd come out and then didn't, those who binged with me, drank to excess with me and took drugs with me had to go. They were a reflection of myself and in order to change that reflection I had to change who I chose to be friends with.

There was a definite backlash to this habit-changing behaviour. My binge eating increased before it moderated. At one point it seemed that everyone in my life was destructive – until the light turned on in my head . . . maybe the problem was *me*. I couldn't go to any of the haunts I used to frequent for fear of confronting an 'ex-friend'. If I saw someone I knew in the street I would cross the road or lower my head in the hope they would not recognise me. I worried what they thought when I no longer returned their calls. At the time I could see no way to deal with my excess other than to excessively cut it out of my life.

The more I said no the more liberated I began to feel. No, it's not okay that you steal my clothes. No, it's not okay that I do your work for you. No, it's not okay that you stood me up for the third time this week.

When I was comfortable with saying no, I found my binge eating did calm down but it did not stop and I needed to address it directly. I ate when I was empty, I ate when I was angry, I ate when I was sad. In order to stop eating I had to deal with the emptiness, express the anger and shed the tears. I could not place limits on my eating for that felt like dieting and dieting always set me up for a binge. No sugar, no fat, no chocolate, all of these restrictions I had placed on my eating needed to be lifted so I brought all these foods into my home, replacing them as they were eaten. By bringing these otherwise illegal foods into my house they eventually lost their mystery. If they were not forbidden the chances were I would not want them as much. I didn't. When the food lost its all-or-nothing appeal my eating moderated and my weight settled.

They say that cigarette smokers experience nicotine cravings once every half hour. When these cravings hit they can last for up to ten minutes. At the end of the ten minutes the craving is no more. It is recommended smokers who want to quit ride the craving through. The more they do this the more confident they become and the less impact the craving has. I had to learn to do this with all my cravings for spending, eating, drinking and smoking. When I rode the craving without giving in to it I realised it was the emptiness that was creating the problem. The spending, eating and drinking were all just symptoms of the cause, self-punishment through gluttony. The cause was the emptiness I felt just from living.

I began to sit with the discomfort of the empty feeling, I learned to acknowledge it and the empty feelings would eventually pass. Sometimes I would still try to fill the hole with food but the feeling wouldn't actually go away until I just sat with it. Sitting with myself meant facing what I had been running from all along: me.

I found I got a buzz from feeling like an adult. I got a buzz from paying my bills on time, managing my money, cooking nutritious meals; I got a buzz from insuring my car, checking the oil, cleaning the oven; I got a buzz from eating blueberry cheesecake with friends on a rainy afternoon, from pillow fights with my boyfriend, from brunch with my parents when I picked up the bill. A grown-up, me a grown-up!

Occasionally I still want to ditch myself – that's when I find myself opening the fridge door in the hope last night's leftovers can help me rid myself of the empty feeling, pouring an extra glass of wine, purchasing a gold-plated dog bowl just in case I ever decide to buy a dog, and wasting my milk money on instant lotteries.

But if we track back the events that led to those compulsive moments then we can usually get to the root of the compulsion. All right, so it's not that easy to stop and take stock when you're eating your way out of the fridge or when you're lying in the beer trough with the floating cigarette butts. But observing our compulsive behaviours is crucial to understanding when and why they happen and understanding how we can make alternative choices that allow us to move forward with our lives.

Here I sit in a restaurant picking at the bread roll that accompanied my friend's pasta. I do not order anything since I have eaten an hour earlier. However, before I can blink I have devoured my friend's entire roll and started on the remains of her pasta. I am day-dreaming of Snickers bars or apple crumbles and can't sit still in my chair. I don't hear what she has to say, I just feel this insatiable discomfort. Then I wonder why I am feeling like this.

I track the discomfort back to a phone call with my mother earlier this morning. I asked her and Dad to come over and take my old wardrobe away to store in their garage.

She had other plans and said she could not do it. I was furious that she said no, I had no concept that she had a life of her own. I felt abandoned and unimportant. Irrational? Yes. Halfway through my friend's cappuccino dregs I realise the source of the compulsion. I borrow my friend's phone, I call my mother and tell her I understand she has a life of her own and I am sorry for expecting her to drop everything in favour of me. I feel better and I no longer need to eat.

If only all compulsive episodes were that easy to track back to the trigger point!

Sometimes our mothers seem like daily reminders of what we could become if we are not careful. A key to my own recovery was accepting my mother as an individual and not someone put on this earth to make my life a misery or service me endlessly. My mum is a cool chick. She's strong, she's courageous, she's got a great sense of humour. I know that now. The plump, friendly, overly generous mother is a reminder that we too could become plump if we give ourselves away. The reed-thin mother with her daily manicures and polished pumps is a reminder that we too had better keep up or we will be left behind. The mother who is our best friend is a reminder that we too will get old and hanker for our youth.

From where I'm sitting it seems the feminism we grew up with never included our own mothers. While we are more than happy to wax lyrical about the lack of powerful jobs for women and the misogynistic behaviour of the corporate male and to support our girlfriends in times of crisis, our mothers are never included in this lyrical female waxing. It is our mothers we are trying to struggle free from. As women we say we want the best for other women but when those women are our mothers they are not included in the equation. 'Women should have access to childcare – but my mother should have stayed at home with me.'

Our mothers envy us as teenagers because we have yet to live by the consequences of our life-forming decisions. We loathe our mothers because they have had to live by those consequences of their own life choices and we swear we shall never do the same. But we do. We can't bear to see their imperfections because they reflect our own. Why do grown women run screaming when they hear their mother's words escape their lips, or see their mother's chin in their mirror? For me it's my mum's knees. I have them and I don't want them.

I grew up in a coven of women. Where we should have been boiling brews, swapping spells and bonding with blood my sisters and I declared war on my mother and attacked one of our own kind. As nasty as we were to our mother, we were always nastier to ourselves. As our bodies sprouted Mum's breasts and child-bearing hips we attacked our flesh, sometimes feeding it in an attempt to cover it up and sometimes starving in an attempt to prevent the inevitable metamorphosis into our maternal parent.

From age eleven my mother turned a blind eye to my disordered eating. While I was bingeing in my bedroom, she bought packets of Tim Tams and put them away where I could find them. She cooked for a family of ten when there were only five and piled our plates high with suet dumplings, Yorkshire pud and lashings of trifle. She paid for me when I joined Jenny Craig, and again when I tried Gloria Marshall and then again when I tried Weight Watchers but she never stopped cooking. She said nothing about the coins missing from her wallet and the empty chocolate wrappers under my bed. She had been beaten by the patented five-step plan so many times she had given up trying to reconcile second helpings with the payments on my diet plan.

I looked at my mother and saw the body I loathed and the woman I would become and I rebelled. I wanted the genetic blessings of my blonde girlfriends whose mothers were stick figures and whose daughters were flat-chested.

My friends' mothers were their best friends, or so it

seemed. At high school I spent hours after school in the kitchens of my girlfriends' homes. Andrea's mum would sit around the table with us and gossip about the girls at school. She'd buy Andrea clothes that Andrea liked, she had an opinion on everything and everyone and I looked at her mesmerised. Gee, if only I could have a mother as fun as you. Andrea's mum was trim, taut and terrific and kept an eye on her own and her children's weight, dieting with them when she felt the need. I just knew if I'd had Andrea's mum as my best friend then my life would have been swell.

If not Andrea's then Katrina's mum, who was hitting tennis balls with her martini friends and was never home when we were munching in her kitchen, who let Katrina stay out late and do cool stuff like have boys over to watch videos. Or Maryanne's mum who had all the dads mesmerised as she handed out cut oranges with her tanned hands at netball on a Saturday. She was a real woman: beautiful, trim and sexual.

The first person I met in this world was my mother. The midwife had left my mother's bedroom to call the doctor and I was born while she was gone. I entered the world alone in a room with just my mum. I spent thirty-odd years doing everything in my power not to be alone with her again. She did nothing wrong. She loved me, fed me, bathed me, cared for me, provided me with all I could want and more.

The perfect mother does not exist. Yeah, yeah, you've heard it all before. So why do we still prefer our friends' mothers to our own? Why do we proclaim we will be the best damn mothers in the world when we talk of our babies to come? Because we still believe in Carol Brady after all. We believe in the perfect mother. Without her we will be forced to accept that we, like our mothers, are flawed and flawed means limits.

I wished for Carol Brady's dress sense, the department store home décor and the manicures of my best friend's mother. Instead I got my own mother's visible panty line, seventies kitsch, bitten nails and overwhelming generosity.

It is far easier to accept the soft focus version of motherhood that Carol Brady represents rather than the screaming, guzzling, overbearing, controlling, crying, manic reality of the mothers we grow up with. But until I can accept, cherish and celebrate that panty line, that kitsch and those bitten nails then I cannot accept the person who stares back at me from the bathroom mirror each morning. The key to self-acceptance for me was mother acceptance. There is no Carol Brady, she does not exist. Mothers are flawed, mothers are women who compete with other women including their daughters, mothers can be alcoholics, chronic dieters, obsessive shoppers. These mothers are no doubt trying to run from their own mother whom they see in their mirrors each morning.

I for one finally woke up to this and no longer believe that the day I walk down the aisle my hair will turn blonde, my thighs disappear and a housekeeper will appear out of nowhere. I know when I have my first child I shall cry from sleep deprivation and curse my mother when my breasts don't produce milk.

But it wasn't just my attitude to my mother that needed work. Scrutiny of all aspects of my life was imperative to my recovery. Holding a mirror up to myself was confronting in itself and I often retreated to the fridge for support. I had to accept myself fully, to be truly aware of what I was doing with my 3 a.m. binges and 4 a.m. bowel torture in order to begin to understand that I did have a choice in the way I lived my life.

My recovery took years. It started with telling my parents in the restaurant in London and is still going on now. Many times I fooled myself that I was getting better and didn't have a problem. Regardless of what you choose to help your recovery, whether it is books, support groups, doctors, medication or yoga, the emotional work still needs to be done. But when you stop fighting the pain or fighting the binge it does all get better, eventually. My obsessive nature ensured that I would recover. I committed to my recovery like I had previously committed to a binge.

The struggle gets easier. The more positive choices I make the more natural they become until they are second nature. I know that I must become aware of what is troubling me and understand why it is troubling me before I can make an effort to change what is troubling me. This takes time.

I had an audition recently for a television show. It came out of the blue and I was given twenty-four hours notice. When I put the phone down after making the appointment time I did not think about it again until the next day. After the audition I went home and got on with other work. It wasn't until hours later that I realised that not once had I thought about my body. In the past I would have starved myself for twenty-four hours, convinced myself I would not get the gig because I was too fat, overcompensated for my imagined obesity, and binged as soon as the audition was over. This time I got the gig. For a fleeting moment I thought, I'll need to get a personal trainer now, but I interrupted that thought before it was finished, knowing that way lies madness. I knew, for I had been down that way before.

I chose a therapist to help me in my journey. Therapy is not for everyone. There are enough alternatives available to find a recovery that will work for you. Courses, weekend workshops, audio tapes and videotapes. The eating or not eating is only a symptom of what is really happening underneath, and finding out what is triggering the symptoms is a painful process. You have to be prepared to listen to your feelings, be aware of your emotions and do some historical sleuthing on your life.

If you are truly prepared to accept the problem and all it encompasses, to look at your life under a microscope and analyse every thought, behaviour and feeling then you are ready to rid yourself of your life-restricting compulsions. This means living a life free of manic obsession, of enjoying each moment and experiencing real love and real life for the first time. This is exciting and worth all the hard work you can put in.

Should you choose therapy to help you discard your obsession, then beware the unqualified counsellor. I once let a counsellor conduct psychological experiments on me, convince me I needed immediate in-house treatment and try to get me to sign away my life savings in order to pay for it. I later found out her only qualification was that she had passed a psychology course by correspondence.

Like obsessions, therapy comes in a variety of flavours. Shop around; you may want to try a couple on for size before choosing the final one.

To help you find your very own therapist I have created a handy list of common terminology to be used for help when interviewing any prospective therapist or counsellor.

ISSUES
What we refer to as 'obsessions' and therapists refer to as 'parents'.

TRIGGERS
Anything that makes you eat, shop, drink, smoke, breathe.

BOUNDARIES
This is what your therapist will spend a lot of time setting up and you will spend a lot of time tearing down.

INAPPROPRIATE BEHAVIOUR
Inviting your therapist out for a candlelit dinner would be considered inappropriate behaviour.

APPROPRIATE BEHAVIOUR
Declining your therapist's invitation to a candlelit dinner would be considered appropriate behaviour.

DISASSOCIATION
This is when you forget to attend your therapy session.

TRANSFERENCE
Blaming your therapist's bills for your inability to pay your MasterCard account would be considered transference of your own financial inadequacy onto your therapist's own greed issues.

FREUD
Austrian psychologist obsessed by his penis.

PENIS ENVY
Anything you bring up in therapy will be considered penis envy. Do not ask why, just accept it as is. Should you feel uncomfortable accepting this it is no doubt your penis envy that is causing the discomfort.

FREUDIAN SLIP
Addressing your therapist as Mum/Dad would be considered a Freudian slip.

PEDESTAL
This is where you will place your therapist for the first ten years of therapy.

DYSFUNCTIONAL
Everyone who is not in therapy.

TIME'S UP
Hand over your cash.

Therapy worked for me and helped me change my life. By understanding why I behaved in a certain manner and realising that behaviour is a choice, I was able to make permanent and positive changes in my life. Having the weekly support of my therapist gave me a support structure my life had previously lacked. Many times I did not want to go to my weekly session. I persevered just the same. When depression enveloped me I increased those sessions to twice a week for almost a year and worked hard at conquering my fears.

Eventually I understood that in order to stop the bingeing I had to take my power back, stop blaming the food and start accepting my own choice to eat. I had to become present when food was in front of me. I had to stop endowing this inanimate object with emotional qualities. The food didn't hate me, the food didn't love me, it didn't invite me to eat it, it had no feelings about me and no emotional investment in whether I chose to eat it or not. It was simply food. As I said, it sounds obvious but try telling that to a woman with a body issue problem.

Once I had done the years of emotional work, 'legalised' all foods and was no longer bingeing I knew it was important to look further at my eating. Why I ate when I did. Who did I eat more with, who did I eat less with? I needed structure around my eating so I went in search of a dietitian, interviewing dozens before I found one who understood the no-diet philosophy. At my first meeting with her she asked me to devise my own food plan and I liked her straight away.

I took responsibility for my eating, looked at what I ate and how it affected me. Stopping dieting was terrifying. Letting go of the rules and beliefs that had held my life together for so long was not an easy process. But I did it. I stopped dieting. I jumped off the Diet Game and I did not die. I stopped believing that a diet would fix my life, that the Perfect Body would save me from the pain of existing in a flawed world, that a bite of chocolate cake could ruin me for life.

At times I fell to pieces, I thought I would never stop eating and believed I would soon be the size of a house. I stuck with it, I committed to never dieting again and I fell to pieces again. But I got there. Through hard work, with emotional support and a lot of information sourced from the Internet and my local bookstore. Stopping dieting opened up a whole new world to me. A world where food and body became incidental and where competition over body does not exist (most of the time!). I began to exercise daily. At first I went walking, outside in the sun enjoying the air. I was tempted to return to my Stairmaster and aerobics class but I resisted, for I knew that path ended in emotional torment and major head spins. My body craved movement and I listened. Gentle, it said, be gentle with me. I took up yoga and was amazed how gentle stretching could change the shape of my body. Another diet myth broken: exercise need not be a chore, nor did it need to be vigorous to make an impact.

I could finally look at my girlfriends and appreciate them for who they were, not judge them for their bodies. I also had to have the courage to let go of those girlfriends stuck on the Diet Game. Diet Pals no longer served a purpose in my new life.

Believe me when I tell you that there is hope for those who are trapped in the confines of a bad diet relationship, stumbling in the race to the finish line and for those of us who communicate in kilojoules, cellulite, BPMs and standard sizing. There's even hope for those of us fed up with controlling Diet Pals, demanding weight loss wenches and pseudo-spouses.

Weight, Weight & Limber are just waiting for your call. Specialising in diet divorce, this firm of competent and reformed diet individuals understands your needs when it comes to the painful split from your diet spouse. They know the heartache involved in dividing the diet books, gym equipment and full-length mirrors. They understand the mud-cake-slinging behaviour that comes with the diet divorce territory. The slander, the lies, 'No, I haven't heard from her, she went off the deep end, started eating chocolate before 8 a.m., she won't come to weight-loss group and I just can't relate to her any more', the 3 a.m. hyperventilating down the phone line and the furtive looks from behind the cardboard crackers in aisle six.

Weight, Weight & Limber offer a complete service in the comfort of your own home, making the diet-divorce process as pain-free as possible. They'll even put you in touch with a support group in your area so you can meet others who have been trapped in a meaningless diet relationship. (And if you call before 6 p.m. tonight you'll receive a free copy of their book *The Breakdown of the Modern Diet Relationship, How to Really Communicate with Your Girlfriends Without Resorting to Weight Watching*.)

'Do you, Rachael Oakes-Ash, promise to keep your hands off Andrea's pie, renege your position on the game board and retire from the race from this day forward?'

'I do.'

'Do you, Andrea, promise to allow Rachael to retire gracefully, and vow never to taunt her with magazine cut-outs of low-fat food, Weight Watchers 2-for-1 meetings and comments on her weight?'

'I do.'

'I now declare this diet divorce legal. You may kiss the scales goodbye.'

'Can't I just throw them in the back of my cupboard? You never know when I might need them again.'

'No. You must kiss the scales goodbye.'

'Oh, all right then, thank you, Your Honour . . . Now do you think you can do something about erasing those Year Seven weight records?'

GOOD GIRLS DO SWALLOW

I AM PROUD OF MY BEAUTIFUL BUTT. It's round, it's plump and it's comfortable. If presented with a bum line-up most women wouldn't choose my bum but I would. Women in Hollywood would diet it off and miss out on its nurturing qualities. Women on the social circuit would pay thousands to have it sucked out. Not for them a bum that has attitude, that says 'Hello, I am here'.

Why is my life considered doomed if I have a fat bum, a wide waist or a flat chest? Why am I forced to try on undersized clothing in changing-rooms with interrogation-room lighting? Why do fourteen-year-old girls advertise anti-ageing cream? What is really wrong with my size fourteen arse? What woman on her deathbed honestly says 'I wish I had dieted more'?

Once upon a time I never believed I could ever have suggested this but it's time for women with big arses, curvaceous tummies, and strong thighs to unite. It's time to reclaim the bum. The bigger the bottoms the more demand for big-behind clothing. The designers will be forced to add extra metres of fabric to their standard ten centimetre pattern. But wait, there's more. We need to encourage salesgirls to eat, to be proud of their arses, to be honest about ours. We need an Arse-In. A collective community of posterior princesses camping out in buttist stores. 'Does my bum look big in this?' will be greeted with a resounding 'Yes, your bum is huuuuuuuuuuge and beautiful'. Bumper stickers with 'The Gluteus Maximus is Groovy' and 'Fat Arse Aboard' will adorn our wide-berth cars. It will be just like the '60s, we'll burn our girdles and let our arses hang free. Oh yes, it will be fabulous.

In my pursuit of the Perfect Body I have downed laxatives and swallowed Ipecac syrup, inhaled thousands of cigarettes, digested speed pills and starved myself. My metabolism was shot the moment I went on my first diet; starving the body only slows the body metabolism down as it enters famine mode. The more you starve the harder it is to lose weight in the long run.

I am one of the lucky ones. I could have ended up infertile from my starvation, but I didn't. My pearly whites could have ended up acid-brown but they didn't. My bowels could have packed it in and I could have found myself using colonic irrigation to help loosen the compacted bowel movements as a result of excessive laxative abuse. I didn't.

I have stretch marks on my breasts and my hips from the constant weight loss and gain. I can't spell to save myself as a result of my time on anti-depressants. My teeth have more cavities than average from the excessive sugar intake. But overall I have my health. When I throw up as a result of a virus I still feel a slight rush at the prospect that I could be losing weight but I would now prefer to be healthy and functional than ill in the bathroom.

At one time I would not have known the Perfect Body if it had sat next to me at lunchtime. If I had it, the mirror told me otherwise. I couldn't have the Perfect Body without Bad Body Image and Bad Body Image prevented me from having the Perfect Body.

If the majority of people have an Imperfect Body (IB), that would make the IB the norm, would it not? If the IB is the norm and no one wants to be different then why do we lust after the abnorm, the PB? When the Rubik's cube came out, everyone wanted one because everyone had one, the same with Donkey Kong, Pokémon and bread-makers. If everyone has an IB, then why are we lusting after the PB? Shouldn't we be happy in the knowledge of our normalcy, or do we have to be abnormal to be happy? I'm getting a headache just thinking about it.

When the Perfect Body is the ideal then life is meaningless without it. The Perfect Body is irrational, unachievable and downright dangerous and life will remain meaningless for those who worship the Perfect Body and for whom it remains the ideal. The variety of bodies on the steps of the amphitheatre should have been enough to show us that there is no 'one size fits all', no Perfect Body.

In puberty we were discovering who we were and defining our identity. We judged ourselves by each other's code of dress, choice of boyfriend and weekend party attire. 'Did you see her at the party in that dress so short, she really thinks she's something? Her legs are so long and thin, does she have to parade them like that?' 'Of course, all the boys like her. Who wouldn't? She puts out, you know,' translated into 'I felt like such a dud at that party. I didn't fit in. My legs are too fat, I don't want to be seen. All the boys hate me'. The obsession with body was so great that we lost ourselves before we even had the chance to discover who we really were.

Dieting kept us from facing our own sprouting sexuality as our bodies developed minds and angles of their own. While we concentrated on each other's bodies and on who had put on weight – 'Angela's thighs are getting a bit big' – who had lost weight – 'how do you think she does it?' – we didn't have to face the screaming in our parents' home, our sister's groping boyfriend or the bleeding we went through each month.

The myth is that if you diet then you are a good girl. Good girls get good jobs, good girls get good-looking boyfriends, good girls get four-bedroom homes with swimming pools, and all because good girls don't swallow. The price to pay for being a good girl is starvation: don't eat and you'll keep the picture-perfect lifestyle.

GOOD GIRLS DO SWALLOW

Newsflash! You don't have to starve to be good. Saying no to breakfast, lunch and dinner makes no difference to the job interview, the wedding, the formal, the first date. You can bet your hot ass that when confronted with your own death you are not going to be wondering where the nearest Jenny Craig outlet is. A terminal illness would bring relief if it meant, 'Oh goodie, I can eat now, it doesn't matter because I am going to die anyway, so I will have that piece of mud cake, thank you, and yes, I would like full cream milk in my coffee.' Well, guess what, we have a terminal illness. It's called life. We all die, whether we diet or not. Dying to a T.

If you want to end up with a healthy body image you have to stop buying into the image fed to you on billboards, television and advertising each day. Throwing out Barbie and refusing to buy high fashion magazines may not be the answer, particularly if you are a growing girl. Human nature says we want what we don't have and removing Barbie from your home doesn't mean you remove the desire for Barbie. Spending time in communal bathhouses and swimming pools may help: looking around and seeing the plethora of body shapes put on this earth. We need to demystify the Perfect Body for the airbrushed, touched-up, digitally enhanced image it is.

How many hours do you think you have wasted with dieting, weight obsession and coveting thy neighbour's flat tummy? How many times have you slaved over a hot treadmill in the gym when the sun was shining outside? How many dates have you refused, beaches have you not swum at and parties have you not gone to because you thought you were fat?

No one has been put on this earth to gratify your emotional needs twenty-four hours a day – not your mother, not your father, not your boyfriend, nor your best friend. You are not the centre of their universe. You will not die if you don't get invited to a party, you will not die if you don't get the job you want, you will not die if you are the fattest girl at the party, and you will not die if your boyfriend leaves you. You may get angry, upset, jealous, petulant or pissed off but life will go on.

There are limits in this world. Everything does come to an end. Relationships finish, holidays don't go on forever, credit cards will only buy so much. Youth moves into middle age and middle age into old age. I will never have the body of a nineteen-year-old again. I am now an adult and with that comes responsibility. It took me thirty years to grow up and accept 'no'.

To this day the word 'no' still at times paralyses me. Who would have thought that a tiny monosyllabic word could have such power and throw me back twenty years to childhood? 'No, Rachael, I won't pick you up from work, or meet you for a drink, or give you a pay rise, or offer you the job, or let you into drama school or serve you a cocktail.' I am frozen with fear and disbelief. Even now I find myself stamping my stilettos and pouting my painted lips, seething and sulking and steaming from my coiffed hair, and resorting to my patented five-step A–E plan to getting what I want. Only in Grown-up Land I don't always get it.

I used to love Carol Brady; now I love my own mother and join in when she says, 'I can't stand that stupid woman'. What woman in her right mind goes to bed with a man like Mike and sews? What woman in her right mind finds a man in cotton pressed pajamas sexy? What woman in her right mind would move into a house with no toilet?

I have hated my parents and my sisters, abhorred myself and screamed at the world. I have wanted to be in anybody else's family but my own. Through years of confrontation, of looking hard at myself and my behaviour, of choosing what is and isn't good for me, of finally only accepting the best of all things in choice of partner, friends and work I have come to love myself and in turn my family. My parents are now a source of phenomenal support. They have stood by me even when I blamed them for everything bad in my life. I know that without them I would not be here, would not have experienced all I have and would not have this story to tell.

My life is not a horror story, it's just my life. Why bemoan the past ten, fifteen, twenty years of my life when I can get on with the next ten, fifteen, twenty years with the rewards of my emotional work? I wouldn't take a moment of my life back, not one. I didn't always feel like that, but I do now.

I could have been an alcoholic or a drug addict or a compulsive gambler. Instead I was a compulsive eater and dieter. I chose to blame my body for all that was wrong with my world. I now know that life is partially about loss and disappointment, that the world isn't always fair. But I am also convinced that life is valuable and to be cherished. Each moment I eat when I am hungry, or when I spend time with my boyfriend without obsessing about the future or revisiting the past, or when I sit opposite my mum at lunch and laugh out loud with her I realise I almost didn't have these things. Knowing what it is like without them makes them worth so much more.

I don't kid myself that the life ahead of me is going to be all roses and no thorns. I have grown up enough to realise that's not the case. But I now have the tools to deal with all that is presented to me and I know I have a lot of joy and love to look forward to. I'm no guru. Once upon a time I would have revelled in the role: adore me, look at me, adore me, look at me. But I know now I don't have all the answers to back it up.

Things don't miraculously get better. It takes work. Nothing will improve until the emotional work is done. When you admit the problem there is amazing relief and a belief that all is well with the world. This is short-lived. The hard work has then to be done.

If you want the answer then you have to look within yourself. I only have the answer for me. I wish I had the right answer for you; I really do. I also wish I could solve world poverty, ban beauty pageants and inject sense into the male-dominated world of advertising and media. The answer starts with swallowing, eating, keeping it down, not throwing it up or eating too much or shitting it out. Knowing what you want, growing up, not being a ten-year-old in a lolly shop saying, 'I want that. No, I want that. No, I want what she's having. No, I want that.'

Who knows if my life would have been different if I had been chosen to do the ballet exam or been born to a blonde, perfect mother or had hit puberty later? A number of factors contributed to the development of my bad body image and eating disorders. I'm an excessive person by nature and conditioning. I come from a long line of excessive women. My inability to balance a cheque book, my shopaholicism, my need to obliterate myself with alcohol and drugs were all just manifestations of my refusal to accept myself and look at the eating disorders that ruled my life. There is no one big moment that can be attributed to my lifelong behaviour. And it is lifelong.

I still eat for comfort; who doesn't? But I no longer beat myself up about it the next day. Chocolate still provides a listening ear when I have PMT and boy, does it taste good. My Visa card hovers between the red and the black but I manage it. I can walk out my front door and not be tempted by the window displays promising me a new life to match the new dress.

Without my disordered eating I am left with the occasional spurt of Bad Body Image. There are still some times that my distorted view of my body rears its ugly head. When I am anxious, or uncertain, or feeling down I can easily see five kilos of excess weight that has miraculously appeared overnight. I usually find that when it happens I am buying into the belief that there is a Perfect Body, that one size does fit all.

It is hard to live in a world surrounded by two-dimensional thin people at every turn and not feel huge on some days. It's usually just a sign that I need to centre myself, that something in my life is askew and it's not my body. I remind myself that changing my body is not going to change my life but changing my thoughts will ensure I drop that five kilos next time I look in the mirror. The thought-changing diet works every time.

At times I miss the binge but my life goes on. I know the

binge isn't going to fix anything, just like I know the man isn't going to fix anything. I don't ask the binge, the man, the job, the clothes to save my life, for I no longer need saving. I am okay as I am. Of course I experience moments of anxiety . . . oh my God, what if he doesn't love me any more, what if she gets the job, or they don't like the book . . . But that's all they are, moments, and moments pass when you let them.

When I find myself hovering around the kitchen or picking at my boyfriend's leftovers I know there is something not quite right with my world. The very act of bingeing is a warning signal to myself; it is me trying to tell me something. *Hello, Rachael, there is something I feel uncomfortable with. I need to express it and the only way right now is to eat. Can you help me?* As soon as I want to or start to binge, be it one biscuit or ten bags of popcorn, I can track it back to a trigger point and give myself the support I need. The binge does not go on and on.

It is impossible for me to put on five kilos in a day. My butt does not miraculously expand by thirty centimetres overnight. It's all in my head. There is also not a set number of thin bodies in this world. I am not stealing someone else's thin body when I get thin and someone else is not stealing mine when I get fat. Competing with other women only prevents me from maintaining honest relationships with those same women. There is enough to go around.

What the diets promised, I got. I got the body that can wear the clothes, I got the job I love, I got the man I want. Except I only got them for keeps when I stopped dieting. Prior to that the glamour lifestyle of hot jobs in the media limelight, famous or rich boyfriends, designer clothes, harbourside apartments meant nothing because I believed I only deserved it if I was thin. Good Girls Do Swallow and get the job, and the car, and the man if that's what the Good Girl wants.

Now I reserve my gluttony for the finer things in life, like writing, playing and making love, and punishment is something I no longer want to know about. If life was a credit card I would be happy with my limit.

When we are born we are all given a slice of pie. This pie is delicious and unique to us. It is our own perfect piece of pie and it is no bigger or smaller than anyone else's. Most of us don't even know we have a slice of pie, let alone what flavour it is, yet we lust after everyone else's. When we are hungry for attention or acknowledgement, it never occurs to us to look inward. We stare outward, wishing for somebody else's slice of pie but not wanting to expose our greed.

I have decided to hold a party, to which you are all invited. Wear your Sunday best and tell all your girlfriends to come. I shall hold it in a tent surrounded by desert. I shall drape red and gold handwoven silks from the floor to the ceiling and scatter cushions on the velvet ground. I am going to bake one giant pie six foot deep with sumptuous filling and sweet. thick crusty pastry. Encased within will be a tempting mix of sexual promise, career fulfilment, friendship and family.

With my silver blade I'll measure and divide it equally, one ginormous slice each, dished up on bone china edged in gold. Everyone will get a solid silver ladle with which to taste their pie. Each slice will be so satisfying in its texture, so enveloping in its aroma that the owner will no longer lust after the other slices. And when gatecrashers and pie thieves arrive, as invariably they will, there will be slices of pie for them too.

You already have that slice of pie. It has everything you will need for nourishment in your life. It is just as good as everyone else's, no better, no worse. Just as tasty. Occasionally you may hit a sour bite but the next will be sweeter, if only by comparison. There is a limit to how much you can ask someone else to taste yours and how much you can taste someone else's. No one else's will give you the satisfaction that your own can supply. So go on, take a bite, savour its flavour, experience the sweetness, the tartness and the comfort. It's good, isn't it? Bet you didn't think it would be this good, did you? Mmmmm, and it's been right in front of you all along. Now all you have to do is swallow.

GOOD GIRLS DO SWALLOW

FIGURES TO DIE FOR

The statistics quoted in the Introduction were found in the following sources.

How many people have dieted
95 per cent of women have dieted at some time.
Liz Dittrich PhD, Director of Research and Outreach, About Face website, San Francisco.

Lost weight regained
95 per cent of dieters regain their lost weight within two years.
Kaz Cooke, *Real Gorgeous: the Truth About Body and Beauty*, Allen and Unwin Australia, 1994.

Age of anorexia sufferers
There are three times as many anorexic women in their twenties and thirties than adolescents.
Healthy Weight Journal 1999:13:3;34 / Pawluck D, Gorey K. 'Secular trends in the incidence of anorexia nervosa', *International Journal of Eating Disorders*, 1998:23; 347–52.

Bulimia developing from anorexia
40 per cent of anorexics will later develop bulimia.
Johnson et al., 'The Syndrome of Bulimia: Review and Synthesis', *Psychiatric Clinics of North America*, 1984, Vol. 7, No. 2, pp. 247–73.

Number of people suffering from eating disorders
There are three times as many people with eating disorders than with AIDS in the United States.
Eating Disorders Awareness and Prevention, Seattle USA, www.edap.org

Who wants to be thinner?
72 per cent of high school girls want to be thinner; 80 per cent think that being thinner is better.
Paxton S J et al., 'Body Image Satisfaction, Dieting Beliefs, and Weight Loss Behaviours in Adolescent Girls and Boys', *Journal of Youth and Adolescence*, 1991, Vol. 20, No. 3, pp. 361–79.

Thin models create depression
Anxiety, stress, depression and self-consciousness increase when viewing thin models.
Healthy Weight Journal 1998:12:4;50 / Kalodner C. 'Media influences on male and female non-eating-disordered college students', *Eating Disorders,* 1997:5:47–57.

Who thinks they are too fat?
75 per cent of women think they are too fat despite being in a healthy weight range.
Glamour Magazine, 1984.

GI Joe beefs up
GI Joe has increased over forty centimetres around his chest.
Healthy Weight Journal 1999:13:5;67 / Pope H, Olivardia R,

Gruber A, et al. 'Evolving ideals of male body image as seen through action toys', *International Journal of Eating Disorders*, 1999:26: 65–72.

Bombarding advertisements
We view 400–600 advertisements a day with conflicting beauty messages.
Liz Dittrich PhD, Director of Research and Outreach, About Face website, San Francisco.

Thin chicks on TV
70 per cent of female TV stars are thin and only 5 per cent overweight.
Liz Dittrich PhD, Director of Research and Outreach, About Face website, San Francisco.

Kids dieting
81 per cent of ten year olds have been on a diet and 40 per cent of nine and ten-year-old girls are trying to lose weight. Eating Disorders Awareness and Prevention, Seattle USA, www.edap.org

Dieting industry
The dieting industry is estimated to be worth over $33 billion worldwide.
Marketdata Enterprises Inc., USA, 1994.

Bulimia brought on by dieting
Bulimia usually occurs during dieting.
Liz Dittrich PhD, Director of Research and Outreach, About Face website, San Francisco.

LEFT-OVERS

BOOKS TO CHEW OVER

All of these books can be ordered through your local bookstore or bought online.

Ball, Jillian; Buttow, Phyllis; Place, Fiona, *When Eating is Everything*, Doubleday, 1991.

Bovey, Shelley, *The Forbidden Body*, Pandora, 1989.

Cohen, Mary Anne, *French Toast for Breakfast*, Gurze, 1995.

Cooke, Kaz, *Real Gorgeous*, Allen & Unwin, 1994.

Devane, Mary; Valentis, Anne, *Female Rage*, Crown Publishers, 1994.

Erdman, Cheri, *Nothing to Lose*, Harper, 1995.

Fraser, Laura, *Losing It*, Plume Scholastic Paperbacks, 1998.

Friday, Nancy, *My Mother My Self*, Delacorte Press, 1977.

Hall, Lindsey, *Full Lives*, Gurze, 1993.

Hall, Lindsey; Cohn, Leigh, *Bulimia: a Guide to Recovery*, Gurze, 1992.

Harris, Di, *Stop Dieting and Lose Weight*, Di Harris, 1999.

Hirschmann, Jane; Munter, Carol, *When Women Stop Hating Their Bodies*, Fawcett, 1997.

Hollis, Judi, *Fat is a Family Affair*, Hazeldon, 1985.

Hornbacher, Marya, *Wasted*, HarperCollins, 1998.

Kano, Susan, *Making Peace with Food*, Amity, 1985.

Maine, Margo, *Father Hunger*, Gurze, 1991.

McFadden, Judith; McFadden, Jenny, *Diet No More!*, Signet, 1995.

Normandi, Carol; Roark, Laurelee, *It's Not About Food*, Grosset, 1998.

Ogden, Jane, *Fat Chance*, Routledge, 1992.

Orbach, Susie, *Fat is a Feminist Issue*, Arrow, 1978.

Orbach, Susie, *Hunger Strike*, Faber, 1986.

Podjasek, Jill, *The Ten Habits of Naturally Slim People*, Contemporary, 1997.

Poulton, Terry, *No Fat Chicks*, Birch Lane, 1997.

Roth, Geneen, *Feeding the Hungry Heart*, Penguin, 1982.

Roth, Geneen, *Why Weight? A Guide to Ending Compulsive Eating*, Penguin, 1989.

Roth, Geneen, *When Food Is Love*, Piatkus, 1991.

Roth, Geneen, *When You Eat at the Refrigerator, Pull Up a Chair*, Hyperion, 1998.

Roth, Geneen, *Breaking Free from Compulsive Eating*, Signet, 1993.

Sark, *Succulent Wild Woman*, Fireside, 1997.

Tebbel, Cyndi, *The Body Snatchers*, Finch, 2000.

Wann, Marilyn, *Fat! So?*, Ten Speed, 1999.

WEBSITES TO SAVOUR

You can find the *Good Girls Do Swallow* website at www.lipschtick.com.au, and I have found the following to be beneficial, informative and entertaining.

ABOUT FACE www.about-face.org/ Combating negative and distorted images of women.

BEYOND HUNGER www.beyondhunger.org The exploration of body hatred through spiritual, emotional and psychological issues.

BODYCAGE www.bodycage.com A recovered anorexic's site.

BODY POSITIVE www.bodypositive.com How to feel good in the body you have.

BODYSCOOP www.bodyscoop.com.au Australia's positive body image website.

BODY TALK www.bodytalkmagazine.com Positive body talk and no fashion police!

BREAKING FREE www.geneenroth.com Geneen Roth's website dedicated to breaking free from disordered eating.

BUST www.bust.com The voice of the New Girl Order! Online girlie zine.

CARING ONLINE www.caringonline.com A great source of websites on body image, eating disorders and dieting.

DIETLESS www.dietless.com Discovering the emotional connection to weight loss.

EATING DISORDERS ASSOCIATION OF QUEENSLAND www.uq.net.au/eda/documents/start.html Australian website offering Australian resources for those experiencing eating anxiety.

FAT! So? www.fatso.com For people who don't apologise for their size.

FULLBLOOM www.fullbloom.com.au Underwear for the real woman.

GURZE BOOKS www.gurze.com US publisher of books on eating disorders and related topics.

HEALTHY WEIGHT NETWORK www.healthyweight.net Exposing diet myths.

HUGS INTERNATIONAL www.hugs.com Dedicated to stopping dieting worldwide.

LARGESSE www.eskimo.com/;sllargesse/ The network for size esteem.

MIRROR-MIRROR www.mirror-mirror.org Informative website offering facts about eating disorders, their symptoms, and support.

MIRROR MIRROR (yes there are two) www.mirrormirror.

com.au Raising awareness of self image and eating issues.

MODE www.modemag.com The new shape in fashion magazines for sizes 12, 14, 16 plus.

ONELIST www.onelist.com Access to online support communities.

RIOTGRRL www.riotgrrl.com Funky girl power website with Feed the Supermodel game!

SOMETHING FISHY WEBSITE FOR EATING DISORDERS www.something-fishy.org Definitions, treatment options, risks, links and bulletin boards for those experiencing eating disorders, and their families.

TEEN OUTREACH www.teenoutreach.com A cool youth portal.

THE BARBIE LIBERATION ORGANISATION www.mse.berkeley. edu/Staff/Eve/barbie.html Liberate Barbie!

THE BODY POSITIVE www.bodypositive.com Australian positive body website for healthy advice on body acceptance.

ORGANISATIONS TO RELISH

The following organisations may help you in sourcing an appropriate support group, counsellor, therapist or treatment.

Anorexia and Bulimia Care (ABC)
Website: www.anorexiabulimia care.co.uk
Telephone: 01695 422 479

Anorexia Bulimia Careline (Northern Ireland)
Telephone: 02890 614440

British Association for Counselling and Psycotherapy
1 Regent Place
Rugby
Warwickshire CV21 2PJ
Website: www.bac.co.uk
Telephone: 01788 550 899

British Psychological Society
Website: www.bps.org.uk

Centre for Eating Disorders (Scotland)
Telephone: 0131 668 3051

Eating Disorders Association
Bryson House
38 Ormeau Road
Belfast 7
Ireland

International Eating Disorder Centre
119–121 Wendover Road
Aylesbury
Bucks HP21 9LW
Telephone: 01296 330557
Website: www.eatingdisorders centre.co.uk

The Irish Eating Distress Centre
6 Marino Mart
Dublin 3
Ireland
Telephone: 00353 1833 3126

National Association for Eating Disorders
54 New Road
Esher
Surrey KT10 9NU

GOOD GIRLS DO SWALLOW

Website: www.eating-disorders.org.uk
Telephone: 01372 469 493

National Eating Disorders Association
Wensum House
103 Prince of Wales Road
Norwich NR1 1DW
Website: www.bac.co.uk
Telephone: 01603 619 090

Overeaters Anonymous Great Britain
Answering service 0700 0784 985

AFTER-DINNER MINTS

Those of you who need to be thanked (and there are many) know who you are and I am indebted to you all for contributing in your own unique way to the completion of this book.

To my friends who took 'no, I can't come out' for an answer; to my family for having the courage to stand by my endeavour; to my flatmates who shared my work space while writing this book – thank you for your patience and understanding.

Big kisses to my girlfriends Isabelle Gagnon, Helen Black, Jackie Engel, Jacky Smith, Yasmin Boland and Wendy Herbert for being true Good Girls. Big hugs to Ewan Campbell for always taking me away from my computer before I crossed over into madness and to Genevieve Michael for her compassion and patience.

More kisses to Alex Brooks, who believed in me and my work and kept my rent paid. Thanks to Merran White for giving me Julia Leigh and Matthew Richardson who ensured I got the contract I wanted and the support I needed.

Heartfelt handshakes to the Australian Society of Authors and the Australia Council for giving me the fabulous Anne

Deveson as a mentor. Thanks to Anne Deveson for her advice in adversity. Thanks to Roland and Stuart at the Writers' Studio where the seed for this book was fertilised and to Linda Bradbury who first encouraged me to write. My tastebuds and tummy bow down to Evelyn and her family at Café Preggos who kept my caffeine intake at an appropriate level to ensure late-night writing sessions.

It is a truly magical experience to work as a team on equal footing. My teammates Hazel Flynn and Roberta Ivers showed me when I was being indulgent and praised me when I was not and I thank them for their professionalism, guidance and humour. Big thanks to Jane Palfreyman for opening the chocolates and getting the ball rolling and to Wendy Blaxland for her editing, passion and detail.

To the team at Mainstream Publishing – Bill Campbell, Sharon Atherton, Deborah Kilpatrick, Clive Hewat, Jess Thompson and Fiona Brownlee – thanks for accepting my input with enthusiasm, for guiding *Good Girls* towards the British audience and for making me feel welcome. Appreciation must also go to Marian Keyes, Kathy Lette, Amy Jenkins, Arabella Weir and Susie Orbach for supporting a girl they hardly knew and a story every woman has.

To Stewart McCure from child Rach, adult Rach and high-maintenance Rach – thanks for the constant supply of roses and all they brought with them.

To Kate. You did it. We did it. I did it. Thank you.

The biggest hugs remain for my family: my Mum, my Dad, my two sisters and their families. Thank you is not enough.

ABOUT THE AUTHOR

Rachael ate her first solids at ten months, said her first word a month later and has been talking between mouthfuls ever since. Her vocal wit has been broadcast across her home country, Australia, as co-host of the number one nightly music countdown and host of her own radio show *The Powder Room*. Rachael's sassy opinions have been sought after on national television panels and as an entertainment reporter, fashion reporter and person on the street for all the major Australian television networks.

After her 'thirty is the new twenty' crisis, Rachael began freelancing as a writer and has been published in *Marie Claire*, *New Woman*, *Cleo*, *B Magazine*, *Minx*, *Women's Health*, the *Sunday Telegraph* and the *Sun Herald*.

Rachael was awarded the Australia Council ASA Mentorship for 1999 for *Good Girls Do Swallow*. It has since been made into an award-nominated documentary featuring Rachael as presenter, producer and writer. Rachael recently produced, wrote and hosted her own one-hour TV special, *Three in a Bed*, on the controversial topic of infidelity.

You can contact Rachael via her website www.lipschtick.com.au and be part of her second book research.